Woodbourne Library
Washington-Centervi
Centerville

Praise for the Previous E
Your Credit Scoi

"It's never been more important to get a firm grip on your credit. Whether you're looking to build your score, better it, or simply understand it, Liz Weston is the ultimate guide."

—**Jean Chatzky**, financial journalist, author, and financial editor for the *Today Show*

"Recommended reading!"

—*Wall Street Journal* Online

"A great credit score can help you finish rich! Liz Weston gives solid, easy-to-understand advice about how to improve your credit fast. Read this book and prosper."

—**David Bach**, bestselling author of *The Automatic Millionaire* and *The Automatic Millionaire Homeowner*

"Excellent book! Insightful, well written, and surprisingly interesting. Liz Weston has done an outstanding job demystifying an often intimidating and frustrating topic for the benefit of all consumers."

—**Eric Tyson**, syndicated columnist and bestselling author of *Personal Finance for Dummies*

"No one makes complex financial information easy to understand like Liz Weston. Her straight talk and wise advice are invaluable to anyone with a credit card or checkbook—and that's just about all of us."

—**Lois P. Frankel**, Ph.D., author of *Nice Girls Don't Get the Corner Office* and *Nice Girls Don't Get Rich*

"In a country where consumers increasingly pay more when they have bad credit, Liz Weston's book provides excellent tips and advice on ways to improve your credit history and raise your credit score. If you just apply one or two of her insightful suggestions, you'll save many times the cost of this book."

—**Ilyce R. Glink**, financial reporter, talk show host, and bestselling author of *100 Questions Every First-Time Home Buyer Should Ask*

Woodbourne Library
Washington-Centerville Public Library
Centerville, Ohio

"Your credit score can save you money or cost you money—sometimes a lot of money. Yet, most people don't even know their scores, much less know how to make them better. Liz Weston can help you fix that. In this easy-to-understand guide, you'll learn how to make sure your score helps you get the best deal on loans and insurance. You can't afford not to read it."

—**Gerri Detweiler**, consumer advocate and co-author of the book *Debt Collection Answers*

Your Credit Score

How to Improve the 3-Digit Number
That Shapes Your Financial Future

Fifth Edition

Liz Weston

Publisher: Paul Boger
Editor-in-Chief: Amy Neidlinger
Editorial Assistant: Kim Boedigheimer
Cover Designer: Alan Clements
Managing Editor: Kristy Hart
Senior Project Editor: Lori Lyons
Proofreader: Apostrophe Editing Service
Indexer: Tim Wright
Senior Compositor: Gloria Schurick
Manufacturing Buyer: Dan Uhrig

© 2016 by Pearson Education, Inc.
Publishing as FT Press
Old Tappan, New Jersey 07675

For information about buying this title in bulk quantities, or for special sales opportunities (which may include electronic versions; custom cover designs; and content particular to your business, training goals, marketing focus, or branding interests), please contact our corporate sales department at corpsales@pearsoned.com or (800) 382-3419.

For government sales inquiries, please contact governmentsales@pearsoned.com.

For questions about sales outside the U.S., please contact international@pearsoned.com.

Company and product names mentioned herein are the trademarks or registered trademarks of their respective owners.

All rights reserved. No part of this book may be reproduced, in any form or by any means, without permission in writing from the publisher.

Printed in the United States of America

First Printing October 2015

ISBN-10: 0-13-421248-7
ISBN-13: 978-0-13-421248-7

Pearson Education LTD.
Pearson Education Australia PTY, Limited
Pearson Education Singapore, Pte. Ltd.
Pearson Education Asia, Ltd.
Pearson Education Canada, Ltd.
Pearson Educación de Mexico, S.A. de C.V.
Pearson Education—Japan
Pearson Education Malaysia, Pte. Ltd.

Library of Congress Control Number: 2015946724

Contents

Acknowledgments

Credit and credit scoring can be a complex subject, which means any journalist trying to cover this area of personal finance needs great sources. I've been extraordinarily fortunate to have found experts who not only knew their fields, but who were willing to spend time helping me understand them, too.

At the top of this list is Craig Watts, former spokesman for Fair Isaac Corp., who invested hours researching and carefully answering my endless questions. Others at Fair Isaac were also generous with their time and expertise, including Ryan Sjoblad, Lamont Boyd, Barry Paperno, Anthony Spauve, Christina L. Goethe and David Shellenberger. VantageScore CEO Barrett Burns and spokesman Jeff Richardson were valuable resources as well.

John Ulzheimer, founder of www.CreditExpertWitness.com, is another of my go-to sources. John has a few decades' experience with credit, including stints at both Fair Isaac and Equifax, which gives him a unique depth of experience and authority.

Special thanks also to credit expert Gerri Detweiler, Robert Hunter of the Consumer Federation of America, Gail Hillebrand of the Consumer Financial Protection Bureau, Deanne Loonin and Robin Leonard at Nolo Press, and the folks at Insurance Information Institute, VISA, and Citibank. Thanks, too, to Beth Givens of the Privacy Rights Clearinghouse and Linda and Jay Foley, formerly of the Identity Theft Resource Center for their insights into credit fraud.

Sam Gerdano, executive director of the American Bankruptcy Institute and U.S. Senator Elizabeth Warren, author of *The Two-Income Trap: Why Middle-Class Mothers and Fathers Are Going Broke*, provided their vast knowledge and perspective about the bankruptcy epidemic in America.

Richard Jenkins, formerly my editor at *MSN Money*, conceived and helped shape the series of bankruptcy stories I wrote for that Web site. The project deepened my understanding of the bankruptcy process and its effect on people and their credit. Thanks, too, to the hundreds who volunteered their personal stories about the often-difficult decision to file.

Then there are the cheerleaders—the people who encouraged me to take on and complete this sometimes daunting project. Leading the charge was my husband, Will Weston, who picked up a lot of slack around the house and encouraged me to return to my computer on those many nights when I would have much rather watched a rerun of *Friends*.

My friend and colleague, Kathy Kristof, gave a realistic assessment of what was in store when juggling family, full-time work, and book writing—but told me to go for it anyway.

My first editor at FT Press, Jim Boyd, instantly understood why this book needed to be written and guided me expertly along its route to completion. He and his staff at FT Press were and are terrific.

Finally, I'd like to thank my readers who generously shared their experiences, opinions, praise, and criticism. Your letters and emails helped shape the information in this book and inspired me to keep digging for answers that could make a real difference in your lives.

About the Author

Liz Weston is an award-winning personal finance columnist who authors the question-and-answer column "Money Talk," which appears in the *Los Angeles Times* and other newspapers throughout the country.

Liz has been a regular commentator on American Public Media's *Marketplace Money* and has contributed to NPR's "Talk of the Nation" and "All Things Considered." She has appeared on *Dr. Phil, Today Show*, and *NBC Nightly News*, and was for several years a weekly commentator on CNBC's *Power Lunch*.

Her advice on credit and finance has been featured in *Consumer Reports, Marie Claire, Parents, Real Simple, Woman's World, Woman's Day, Good Housekeeping, Family Circle*, and many other publications.

Formerly a personal finance writer for the *Los Angeles Times*, Weston has won numerous reporting awards, including the 2010 Betty Furness Consumer Media Award by the Consumer Federation of America, designed to honor individuals who have made "exceptional progress in American consumerism."

Her other books include *The 10 Commandments of Money*, which *The New York Times* praised as "a wonderful basic personal finance book... [with] enough counterintuitive ideas to keep even people who know a bit about personal finance reading further." She is also the author of *Deal with Your Debt, Easy Money*, and *There Are No Dumb Questions About Money*, all published by Pearson.

Weston is a graduate of the certified financial planner training program at University of California, Irvine. She lives in Los Angeles with her husband and daughter. She can be reached via the "Contact Liz" form on her Web site, AskLizWeston.com.

Introduction

You have more power than ever before to shape your credit—and your financial future.

Twenty years ago, you didn't even have the right to know the numbers that lenders used to judge you. Today, you can get dozens of your scores online within seconds, along with detailed information about what goes into creating each one. Instead of having too little information, sometimes it can feel like you have too much, to the point where it's difficult to know what's truly important and what you can ignore.

That's where this book comes in. My goal is to help you get the scores you need to live a successful, financially responsible life without having to spend half that life learning about the process.

People's hunger to learn about credit scoring helped make previous editions of this book into national best-sellers. The book you have in your hands now has been completely updated to reflect current laws, trends, and lending practices. It gives you everything you need to know about how to protect your scores if they're high and improve them if they're not.

Now more than ever, knowing how to fix, improve, and protect your credit score is essential for successfully navigating your financial life.

1

Why Your Credit Score Matters

In recent years, a simple three-digit number has become critical to your financial life.

This number, known as a credit score, is designed to predict the possibility that you won't pay your bills. Credit scores are handy for lenders, but they can have enormous repercussions for your wallet, your future, and your peace of mind.

How Your Credit Scores Affect You

If your credit scores are high enough, you'll qualify for a lender's best rates and terms. Your mailbox will be stuffed with low-rate offers from credit card issuers, and mortgage lenders will fight for your business. You'll get great deals on auto financing if you need a car, home loans if you want to buy or improve a house, and small business loans if you decide to start a new venture.

If your scores are low or nonexistent, however, you'll enter a no-man's land where mainstream credit is all but impossible to come by. If you find someone to lend you money, you'll pay high rates and fat fees for the privilege. A bad or even mediocre credit score can easily cost you tens of thousands and even hundreds of thousands of dollars in your lifetime.

You don't even have to have tons of credit problems to pay a price. Sometimes all it takes is a single missed payment to knock more than 100 points off your credit score and put you in a lender's higher risk category.

And we aren't just talking about loans. Landlords, insurers, wireless carriers, and utilities, among others, also use credit-based scores to evaluate applicants and determine deposits. A good score can save you money; a bad score can make life more expensive and difficult.

Yet too many people know far too little about credit scores and how they work. Here's just a sample of the kinds of emails and letters I get every day from people puzzling over their credit:[1]

"I just closed all of my credit card accounts trying to improve my credit. Now I hear that closing accounts can actually hurt my score. How can I recover from this? Should I try to reopen accounts so that I can have a higher amount of available credit?" Hallie in Shreveport, LA

"How do you get credit if you don't have it? I keep getting turned down, and the reason is always 'insufficient credit history.' How can I get a decent credit score if I don't have credit?" Manuel in San Diego, CA

"I am a 25-year-old male who made a few bad credit decisions while in college, as many of us do. I need to improve my credit drastically so I do not continue to get my eyes poked out on interest. What can I do to boost my credit score fast?" Stephen in Dallas, TX

"I joined a credit-counseling program because I was in way over my head. But my wife and I plan on buying a house within the next three years, and she has expressed concern that my participation in this debt management program could hurt my credit score. What should I do to help my overall chances with the mortgage process and get the best rate possible?" Paul in Lodi, NJ

"I'm 33 and have never had a single late payment or credit issue in my life. Yet, my credit score isn't as high as I thought it would be. What does it take to get a perfect score?" Brian in South Bend, IN

---

[1]   As with other real-life anecdotes in this book, the writers' anonymity has been protected and their messages might have been edited for clarity.

What these readers sense, and what credit experts know, is that ignorance about your credit score can cost you. Sometimes people with great scores get offered lousy loan deals but don't realize they can qualify for better terms. More often, people with bad or mediocre credit get approved for loans, but don't realize the high price they're paying.

What It Costs Long Term to Have Poor or Mediocre Credit Scores

If you need an example of exactly how much credit scores can matter, let's examine how these numbers affect two friends, Emily and Karen.

Both women got their first credit card in college and carried an $8,000 balance on average over the years. (Carrying a balance isn't smart financially, but unfortunately, it's an ingrained habit with many credit card users.)

Emily and Karen also bought new cars after graduation, financing their purchases with $20,000 auto loans. Every seven years, they replaced their existing cars with new ones until they bought their last vehicles at age 70.

Each bought her first home with $350,000 mortgages at age 30, and then moved up to a larger house with $450,000 mortgages after turning 40.

Neither has ever suffered the embarrassment of being rejected for a loan or turned down for a credit card.

But here the similarities end.

Emily was always careful to pay her bills on time, all the time, and typically paid more than the minimum balance owed. Lenders responded to her responsible use of credit by offering her more credit cards at good rates and terms. They also tended to increase her credit limits regularly. That allowed Emily to spread her credit card balance across several cards. All these factors helped give Emily excellent credit scores. Whenever a lender tried to raise her interest rate, she would politely threaten to transfer her balance to another card. As a result, Emily's average interest rate on her cards was 9.9 percent.

Karen, by contrast, didn't always pay on time, frequently paid only the minimum due, and tended to max out the cards that she had. That made lenders reluctant to increase her credit limits or offer her new cards. Although the two women owed the same amount on average, Karen tended to carry larger balances on fewer cards. All these factors hurt Karen's credit—not enough to prevent her from getting loans, but enough for lenders to charge her more.

Karen had much less negotiating power when it came to interest rates. Her average interest rate on her credit cards was 19.9 percent.

Credit Cards

	Emily	**Karen**
Credit score	760	660
Interest rate	9.90%	19.90%
Annual interest costs	$792	$1,592
Lifetime interest paid	$39,600	$79,600
Karen's penalty		$40,000

Emily's careful credit use paid off with her first car loan. She got the best available rate, and she continued to do so every time she bought a new car until her last purchase at age 70. Thanks to her lower credit score, Karen's rate was three percentage points higher.

Auto Loans

	Emily	**Karen**
Credit score	760	660
Interest rate	4.25%	8.25%
Monthly payment	$371	$408
Interest cost per loan	$2,235	$4,475
Lifetime interest paid	$17,880	$35,804
Karen's penalty		$17,924

The differences continued when the women bought their houses. During the ten years that the women owned their first homes, Emily paid $34,000 less in interest.

Mortgage 1 ($350,000)

	Emily	**Karen**
Credit score	760	660
Interest rate	4.38%	5.38%
Monthly payment	$1,749	$1,961
Total interest paid (10 years)	$139,057	$173,222
Karen's penalty		$34,165

Karen's interest penalty only grew when the two women moved up to larger houses. Over the 30-year life of their mortgages, Karen paid nearly $100,000 more in interest.

Mortgage 2 ($450,000)

	Emily	**Karen**
Credit score	760	660
Interest rate	4.38%	5.38%
Monthly payment	$2,248	$2,241
Total interest paid (30 years)	$359,319	$406,807
Karen's penalty		$98,338

Karen's total lifetime penalty for less-than-stellar credit? More than $190,000.

If anything, these examples underestimate the true financial cost of mediocre credit:

- The interest rates in the examples are relatively low in historical terms. Higher prevailing interest rates would increase the penalty that Karen pays.

- Karen probably paid insurance premiums that were 20 percent to 30 percent higher than Emily's, and she might have had more trouble finding an apartment, all because of her credit.

- The examples don't count "opportunity cost"—what Karen could have achieved financially if she weren't paying so much more interest.

Because more of Karen's paycheck went to lenders, she had less money available for other goals: vacations, a second home, college educations for her kids, and retirement.

In fact, if Karen had been able to invest the extra money she paid in interest instead of sending it to banks and credit card companies, her savings might have grown by a whopping $2 million by the time she was 70.

With so much less disposable income and financial security, you wouldn't be surprised if Karen also experienced more anxiety about money. Financial problems can take their toll in innumerable ways, from stress-related illnesses to marital problems and divorce.

So, if you've ever wondered why some families struggle while others in the same economic bracket seem to do just fine, the answers typically lie with their financial habits—including how they handle credit.

How Credit Scoring Came into Being

The question remains: How did one little number come to have such an out-sized effect on our lives?

Credit scoring has been in widespread use by lenders for several decades. By the end of the 1970s, most major lenders used some kind of credit-scoring formulas to decide whether to accept or reject applications.

Many were introduced to credit scoring by two pioneers in the field: engineer Bill Fair and mathematician Earl Isaac, who founded the firm Fair Isaac in 1956. Over the years, the pair convinced lenders that mathematical formulas could do a better job of predicting whether an applicant would default than even the most experienced loan officers.

A formula wasn't as subject to human whims and biases. It wouldn't turn down a potentially good credit risk because the applicant was the "wrong" race, religion, or gender, and it wouldn't accept a bad risk because the applicant was a friend.

Credit scoring, aided by ever more powerful computers, was also fast. Lending decisions could be made in a matter of minutes, rather than days or weeks.

Early on, each company had its own credit-scoring formula, tailored to the amount of risk it wanted to take, its history with various types of borrowers, and the kind of people it attracted as customers. The factors that fed into the formula varied, but many took into account the applicant's income, occupation, length of time with an employer, length of time at an address, and some of the information available on his or her credit report, such as the longest time that a payment was ever overdue.

These calculations took place behind the scenes, invisible to the consumer and understood by a relatively small number of experts and loan executives.

The cost to develop and implement these custom formulas was—and still is—considerable. It was not unusual to spend $100,000 or more and take 12 months just to set one up. In addition, not every creditor had a big enough database to work with, especially if the company wanted to branch out into a new line of lending. A credit card lender that wanted to start offering car loans, for example, might find that its database couldn't adequately predict risk in vehicle lending.

That led to credit scores based on the biggest lending databases of all—those held at the major credit bureaus, which include Equifax, Experian, and TransUnion. Fair Isaac developed the first credit bureau-based scoring system in the mid-1980s, and the idea quickly caught on.

Instead of basing its calculations on any single lender's experience, this type of scoring factored in the behavior of literally millions of borrowers. The model looked for patterns of behavior that indicated a borrower might default, as well as patterns that indicated a borrower was likely to pay as agreed. The score evaluated the consumer's history of paying bills, the number and type of credit accounts, how much available credit the customer was using, and other factors.

This credit-scoring model was useful for more than just accepting or rejecting applicants. Some lenders decided to accept higher-risk clients but to charge them more to compensate for the greater chance that they might default. Lenders also used scores to screen vast numbers of borrowers to find potential future customers. Instead of waiting for people to apply, credit card companies and other lenders could send out reams of preapproved offers to likely prospects.

How Credit Use Has Changed over the Years

Credit scoring is one of the reasons why consumer credit absolutely exploded in the 1990s. Lenders felt more confident about making loans to wider groups of people because they had a more precise tool for measuring risk. Credit scoring also allowed them to make decisions faster, enabling them to make more loans. The result was an unprecedented rise in the amount of available consumer credit. Here are just a few examples of how available credit expanded during that time:

- The total volume of consumer loans—credit cards, auto loans, and other nonmortgage debt—more than doubled between 1990 and 2000, to $1.7 trillion.

- The amount of credit card debt outstanding rose nearly three-fold between 1990 and 2002, from $173 billion to $661 billion.

- Home equity lending soared from $261 billion in 1993 to more than $1 trillion ten years later.

Credit scoring got a huge boost in 1995. That's when the country's two biggest mortgage-finance agencies, Fannie Mae and Freddie Mac, recommended lenders use FICO credit scores, which is what Fair Isaac called its groundbreaking score. Because Fannie Mae and Freddie Mac purchase more than two-thirds of the mortgages made, their recommendations carry enormous weight in the home loan industry.

The recommendations are also what finally began to bring credit scoring to the public's attention.

If you've ever applied for a mortgage, you know it's a much more involved process than getting a credit card. When you apply for a credit card, you typically fill out a relatively brief form, submit it, and get your answer back quickly—sometimes within seconds, if you're applying online or at a retail store. The process is highly automated, and there typically isn't much personal contact.

Contrast that with a mortgage. Not only do you have to provide a lot more information about your finances, but getting a home loan also requires that you have ongoing personal contact with a loan officer or mortgage broker. You might be asked to clarify something in your application, be told to supply more information, or be given updates about how your request for funds is being received.

Consumer's Fight for Truth About Credit Scores

It was in the course of those conversations that an increasing number of consumers started hearing about FICOs and credit scores. For the first time, people learned that the reason they did or didn't get the loan they wanted was because of a three-digit number. It became obvious that lenders were putting a lot of stock in these mysterious scores.

But when consumers tried asking for more details, they often hit a brick wall. Fair Isaac, the leader in the credit-scoring world, wanted to keep the information secret. The company said it worried that consumers wouldn't understand the nuances of credit scoring, or they would try to "game the system" if they knew more. Fair Isaac feared that its formulas would lose its predictive capability if consumers started changing their behavior to boost their scores.

Now, some sympathetic mortgage officials didn't buy into Fair Isaac's company line. They thought consumers deserved to know their score, and these officials also often tried to explain how the numbers were created.

Unfortunately, because Fair Isaac wouldn't disclose the formula details, a lot of these explanations were dead wrong. Even more unfortunately, some loan officers perpetuated these myths about credit scoring, even as we learned much more information about what goes into them. (You'll read more about these myths in Chapter 5, "Credit-Scoring Myths.")

Resentment about the secret nature of credit scores came to a head in early 2000. That's when one of the then-new breed of Internet lenders, E-Loan, defied Fair Isaac by letting consumers view their FICO credit scores. For about a month, people could actually take a peek at their scores online and learn some rudimentary information about what the numbers meant. Some 25,000 consumers took advantage of the free service before E-Loan's source for credit-scoring information was cut off.

But the proverbial cat was out of the bag. A few months later, with consumer advocates demanding disclosure and lawmakers drafting legislation requiring it, Fair Isaac caved. It posted the 22 factors affecting a credit score on its Web site, grouped into the five categories you'll read about in the next chapter. Shortly after that, the company partnered with credit bureau Equifax to provide consumers with their credit scores and reports for a $12.95 fee.

In late 2003, Congress finally got around to passing a law that gave people a right to see their scores. By the time this update to the Fair Credit Reporting Act was signed into law, however, access to credit scores was already a fact.

Consumers' access to credit scores was further expanded in 2011, when a portion of the Dodd-Frank financial reform bill kicked in that required lenders to disclose credit scores to applicants.

Credit Controversies

Controversies over credit scoring continue to rage. Here are just of few of them.

Credit Scoring's Vulnerability to Errors

No matter how good the mathematics of credit scoring, it's based on information in your credit report—which may be, and frequently is, wrong. Sometimes the errors are small or irrelevant, such as when your credit file lists a past employer as a current employer. Other times the problems are significant, such as when your file contains accounts that don't belong to you. Many people discover this misinformation only after they've been turned down for credit.

The credit bureaus handle billions of pieces of data every day, so to some extent errors, outdated information, and missing information are inevitable—but the credit-reporting system often makes it difficult to get rid of errors after you spot them.

The rise in automated lending decisions means a human might never see your application or notice that something's awry. The explosion in identity theft, with its millions of victims a year, means more bad, fraudulent information is included in innocent people's credit files every day.

Patricia of Seattle, Washington, tells of the ongoing horror of becoming a victim:

"I've always been careful about protecting my identity. Unfortunately, when I was trying to purchase a home, the real estate broker, to whom I'd given my application with birth date and Social Security number, had her laptop stolen. My worst fears came true when, four months later, I suddenly had creditors calling me like crazy asking why I wasn't paying on accounts that were just recently opened in my name. On top of this, I learned the criminals had also stolen my mail with preapproved credit cards. This has created a nightmare of time, work, and frustration trying to clean up my credit history. It's been over two years now, and I'm still working with the major credit-reporting agencies as we speak."

Credit Scoring's Complexity

You're being judged by the formula, so shouldn't it be easy to understand and predictable? Not even credit-scoring experts can always forecast in advance how certain behaviors will affect a score. Because the formula takes into account so many variables, the best answer they can muster is, "It depends."

The variety of different scoring formulas and different approaches among lenders can confuse matters even further.

Lenders can get scores calculated from different versions of the FICO formula, as well as formulas that have been modified for auto or bankcard lenders, for example. They also can have in-house formulas that incorporate a FICO score along with other information that might punish or reward certain behaviors more heavily than the FICO formula does on its own. Some call the result a FICO score, even though that's not technically correct.

Not surprisingly, this causes confusion for consumers and mortgage professionals alike.

A. J. Cleland, an Indianapolis mortgage broker, discovered how different scores could be when trying to help a client who had been turned down for a loan by a bank. The bank reported the client's FICO score was 602, whereas the FICO score Cleland pulled for the client—on the same day and from the same credit bureau—was 31 points lower:

> *"I called my credit provider and was informed that there are different types of reports and different scores," Cleland said. "I thought your score was your score, period."*

Credit Scoring's Use for Noncredit Decisions

I mentioned earlier that many businesses might check your credit and your credit score when evaluating your application; however, the most controversial noncredit use of scoring is in insurance.

Insurers have discovered an enormously strong link between the quality of your credit and the likelihood you'll file a claim. They can't really explain it, but every large study of the issue has confirmed that this link exists. The worse your credit, the more likely you will cost an insurer money. The better your credit, the less likely you are to have an accident or otherwise suffer an insured loss.

As a result, most homeowners and auto insurers use credit scoring to decide who to cover and what premiums to charge them.

That outrages many consumers and consumer advocates who don't see a logical connection between credit and insurance. Julie, a city worker in Poulsbo, Washington, saw her insurances soar after a divorce and subsequent bankruptcy trashed her credit:[2]

> *"I have had the same insurer for 30 years, never been late, never missed a payment, never had an accident, and never filed a claim—yet now I pay the price of higher rates. I absolutely do not understand how this is fair."*

This leads to another controversy, spelled out in the next section.

Credit Scoring's Potential Unfairness

Developers of credit scoring point out their formulas are designed not to discriminate. Credit scores don't factor in your income, race, religion, ethnic background, or anything else that's not on your credit report.

---

[2] Like many divorced people, Julie discovered that her ex still had the power to trash her credit long after the marriage was over. His unpaid bills, run up on once-joint accounts, showed up on her credit report and ultimately led her to file bankruptcy.

But it's not clear whether the result of those formulas actually is non-discriminatory. Some consumer advocates worry that some disadvantaged groups might suffer disproportionately as a result of credit scoring.

Among their theories: People who have low incomes or who live in some minority neighborhoods might have less access to mainstream lenders and thus have worse credit scores. The lenders these disadvantaged populations do use—finance companies, subprime lenders, and community groups—might not report to credit bureaus, making it harder to build a credit history. If these lenders do report to the bureaus, their accounts might count for less in the credit-scoring formula than those of mainstream lenders. Seasonal work is also more prevalent in some neighborhoods, which can lead to a higher rate of late payments in the off-seasons.

Even if credit scoring doesn't discriminate against groups, it might discriminate against you.

No credit-scoring system is perfect. Lenders know that their formulas will reject a certain number of people who actually would have paid their bills. Another group will be accepted as good risks but then default.

If these groups get too large, the lender has trouble. When too many bad applicants are accepted, the lender's profits plunge. When too many good applicants are rejected, the lender's competitors can scoop them up and make more money.

But lenders accept a certain number of misclassified applicants as a cost of doing business. That's little comfort to you, if you're one of the responsible ones who loses out on the mortgage you need to buy a home, or if you end up paying more for it.

Did Credit Scoring Cause the Financial Crisis?

Critics have pointed to the failure of credit-scoring formulas, especially FICO, to predict soaring default rates as evidence the scores don't work.

Fair Isaac has responded that credit scores were designed to be part of a larger decision-making system, with lenders also taking into account other factors such as the borrower's income, assets, other debts, and ability to repay the loan in question.

Indeed, as far back as 2005, acting U.S. Comptroller of the Currency Julie Williams warned lenders that they were relying too much on "risk-factor shortcuts," such as credit scores that focus on past credit performance, without considering the borrowers' ability to pay the new debt they were taking on.

Lenders paid little heed and in fact continued to lower the scores they found acceptable. By the peak of the mortgage boom in the Fall of 2006, many had stopped bothering to verify borrowers' income or assets. What's more, loan approvals were often based on the borrowers' supposed (but unproven) ability to cover only the initial payments, not the much higher amount that would come due when the variable-rate mortgage rates inevitably adjusted higher.

Similar trends could be seen in auto lending, where some auto finance companies stopped asking about incomes at all, and in credit cards, where issuers continued extending credit limits to people who already carried debt that was greater than what they earned in a year.

Since the credit implosion, newly chastened lenders have once again begun to consider factors other than FICOs, but they have not abandoned credit scores as a crucial part of their decision-making process.

Given all the problems with credit scoring, it's understandable that some people think the system is fatally flawed. Some of my readers tell me they're so angry about scoring and the behavior of lenders in general that they've cut up their credit cards and are determined to live a credit-free life.

The rest of us, though, live in a world where credit is all but a necessity. Few of us can pay cash for a home, and many need loans to buy cars. Credit can help launch or expand a business or pay for an education. And most Americans like the convenience of using credit cards. Although it's true that improper use of credit can be disastrous, credit properly used can enhance your life.

If we want to have credit, we need to know how credit scoring works. Knowledge is power, and the tools I give you in this book will help you take control of your credit and your financial life.

2

How Credit Scoring Works

The first thing you need to know about your credit score is that you don't have *a* credit score: You have many, and they change all the time.

Credit scores are designed to be a snapshot of your credit picture—typically, the picture contained in your credit report. New information is constantly added to your report, and old information is deleted. Those changes can affect your score.

That can be good news or bad news. The good news is that if you have a bad score now, you're not stuck with it forever. You can do a lot to improve your situation and make yourself more creditworthy in lenders' eyes.

The bad news is that you can't rest on your laurels. When you have a good score, you need to constantly monitor your credit to make sure it stays that way.

You also should know that there's more than one credit-scoring system out there. In fact, currently more than 100 credit-scoring models are marketed to lenders.

That said, the best-known credit score brand is the FICO, which was created by a company called Fair Isaac. You're much more likely to be affected by a FICO score than any other type of credit score. FICO is the industry leader. It's used in literally billions of lending decisions each year, including the vast majority of mortgage-lending assessments.

That's why the information in this chapter and elsewhere is based on how the FICO formula calculates your score. Other formula designs might differ somewhat in their details, but the behaviors that help and hurt your score are fairly consistent across the various systems.

Here are some other facts about credit scoring that you should keep in mind:

- **You need to have and use credit to have a credit score—** FICO credit score formulas need at least one account on your credit report that has been open for six months and one account that's been updated in the past six months. (It can be the same account.) If your credit history is too thin, or you've stopped using credit for a period of time, there might not be enough current data in your file to create a regular credit score. That doesn't mean you can't be "scored." Various companies, including Fair Isaac, have developed alternative scores for lenders who want to evaluate people with thin or nonexistent credit histories. To get access to mainstream credit, however, you typically need to have a credit score.

- **A credit score usually isn't the only thing lenders consider—**In mortgage-lending decisions, in particular, lenders may weigh a lot of other information, including your employment history and stability, the value of the property you're buying or refinancing, your income, and your total monthly debt payments as a percentage of that income, among other factors.

  So, although credit scores can be a powerful force in lending decisions, they might not be the sole determinant of whether you get credit.

- **Credit-scoring systems were designed for lenders, not consumers—**In other words, scores weren't created to be easy to understand. The actual formulas, and many of the details of how they work, are closely guarded trade secrets.

The credit-scoring companies don't want the process to be entirely transparent or predictable, as discussed in the preceding chapter. They fear that letting out too many details would allow competitors to copy their formulas. They also worry that their formulas would lose their capability to predict risk if consumers knew exactly how to beat them.

We know more about the formulas than ever before and certainly enough for you to improve your score. But given the number of variables involved and the mystery still surrounding credit scoring, you may not forecast exactly how every action will affect a score, or how quickly.

What Is a Good Score?

One of the first questions many people have about credit scoring is what score lenders consider "good." There is, however, no single answer to that question.

Generally, of course, the higher the score, the better. Each lender makes its own decision about where to draw the line, based on how much risk it wants to take and how much profit it thinks it can make with a given blend of customers. Many lenders don't have a single cutoff but may have many, with each segment qualifying for different rates and terms. Finally, as noted earlier, a credit score is usually only one factor in the lending decision. Although scores typically have a big influence, a lender might decide that other factors are more important.

You can see from this national distribution chart of FICO credit scores that more than one-half of the U.S. population has a FICO score of 700 or higher. Many lenders use 720 or 740 as the cutoff for giving borrowers their best rates and terms. Many also use 660, 640, or 620 as cutoff points. Companies that deal with borrowers below that level are often called "subprime" lenders because their riskier borrowers are considered less than "prime."

Score	Percentage with Score
300–499	4.6%
500–549	7.3%
550–599	8.8%
600–649	9.7%
650–699	13.8%
700–749	19.9%
750–799	17.6%
800–850	18.3%

The Great Recession of 2008 had a huge impact on the credit scoring world. More people fell into the lower brackets (25 percent had scores under 600 in October 2010, compared to 15 percent in 2006), and lenders tightened their standards. As the economy slowly recovered, so did people's scores. As of 2015, 20.7 percent have scores below 600.

Your Credit Report: The Building Blocks for Your Score

Because your score is constructed from the information in your credit report, it's worth looking at what you'll find there.

In addition to identifying information about you—your name, address, and Social Security number—your report lists the following:

- **Your credit accounts**—Sometimes called "trade lines," these include loans, credit cards, and other credit accounts you've opened. Your report lists the type of account, how long ago you opened it, your balances, and details of your payment history.

- **Requests for your credit**—These are known as "inquiries," and there are basically two kinds: hard and soft. When you apply for credit, you authorize the lender to view your credit history. This is known as a "hard inquiry" and can affect your credit score. You might also see inquiries that you didn't initiate. These "soft inquiries" are typically made when a lender orders your credit report to make you a preapproved credit offer. Such marketing efforts don't affect your score. It's also considered a soft inquiry when you check your own reports and scores. Again, there's no impact on your scores.

- **Public records and collections**—These can include collection accounts, bankruptcies, tax liens, foreclosures, wage garnishments, lawsuits, and judgments.

Public records are culled from state and county courthouses. Lenders or collection agencies report most of the other information in your report.

This data is collected, stored, and updated by credit bureaus, which are private, for-profit companies. The three major credit bureaus are Equifax, Experian (formerly known as TRW), and TransUnion, and their business is selling information about you to lenders.

Because they're competitors, the bureaus typically don't share information, and not all lenders report information to all three bureaus. In fact, if you get copies of your credit reports from the bureaus on the same day, you're likely to notice at least a few differences among them. An account that's listed on one credit bureau's report might not show up on the others, for example, or the balances showing on your various accounts might differ from bureau to bureau.

Because your score is based on the information that's in your report at a given credit bureau, the number differs depending on which bureau's credit report is used.

Also, each time you or a lender "pulls" your score (in other words, orders a score to be calculated), it's likely to be at least somewhat different because the information on which it's based probably has changed. Fair Isaac says most people's scores don't change all that much in a short period, but about 25 percent of consumers can expect to see their scores at a single bureau vary by more than 20 points over a three-month stretch.

There are time limits to what can appear on your credit report. Although positive information can appear indefinitely, negative marks—late payments, collection actions, and foreclosures—by federal law generally must be removed after seven years. Bankruptcies can be reported for ten years. Inquiries should be deleted in two years.

How Your Score Is Calculated

When most of us think of scores, we think of the relatively straightforward systems used in sports or in school tests. You get points (and possibly demerits) for certain actions, behaviors, or answers, and those are totaled to determine your score.

Credit scoring isn't nearly so easy. Credit-scoring models use "multivariate" formulas. That basically means that the value of any given bit of information in your report might depend on other bits of information.

To understand how this works, let's use a noncredit example. Suppose that your sister calls you to report that her husband is more than an hour late in coming home from work, and she asks whether you think he's having an affair. To answer the question, you would need to review what you know about this man, including his attitude about his family, his general moral standards, and whether he's had dalliances in the past. Using all these variables, you could try to predict whether your brother-in-law is likely to be stepping out—or might just have stopped off to buy his wife an anniversary present.

Let's suppose that your brother-in-law is a stand-up guy. But you've personally observed your neighbor in a clinch with a woman who was not his wife. If your neighbor was an hour late in coming home and *his* wife asked you your opinion of his likely faithfulness, you might reach quite a different conclusion. So the same behavior—coming home late—could evoke two different predictions based on the information at your disposal.

The number of factors that the FICO formulas evaluate is infinitely greater, so you can see how difficult it can be sometimes to predict the outcomes of certain behaviors.

There's one thing that's always true, though: The FICO model is set up to place more value on current behavior than on past behavior. That means that the effect of your old credit troubles lessens over time if you start handling credit more responsibly.

However, the scores are also designed to react strongly to any signs that a once-good risk might be turning bad. That's why someone with good scores suffers more heavily from a late payment than someone with mediocre or bad scores.

It's generally a lot easier to lose points on your score than it is to gain them back, which is why it's so important to know how to improve and protect your score.

The Five Most Important Factors

Now that you understand in general how credit scores are calculated, we can move on to some specifics. The following are the five main factors that affect your FICO score according to their relative level of importance, along with a percentage figure that reflects how heavily that factor is weighed in calculating FICO scores for the general population. Each factor might weigh more or less heavily in your individual score, depending on your credit situation.

Your Payment History

This makes up about 35 percent of the typical score. It makes sense: Your record of paying bills says a lot about how responsible you are with credit. Lenders want to know whether you pay on time and how long it's been since you've been late, if ever.

To put this in perspective: About one-half of Americans don't have a single late payment on their credit reports, according to Fair Isaac, and only four in ten have ever been 60 days or more overdue in the past seven years.

When it comes to negative marks like late payments, the score focuses on three factors:

- **Recency**—This is how recently the borrower got into trouble. The more time that's passed since the credit problem, the less it affects a score.

- **Frequency**—As you might expect, someone who has had just one or two late payments typically looks better to lenders than someone who has had a dozen.

- **Severity**—There's a definite "hierarchy of badness" when it comes to your credit score. A payment that's 30 days late isn't considered as serious as one that's 60 or 120 days late. Collections, tax liens, and bankruptcy are among the biggest black marks.

If you've never been late, your clean history will help your score. But that doesn't mean you'll get a "perfect" score. A good credit history involves a lot more.

How Much You Owe

This equates to 30 percent of your score. The score looks at the total amount owed on all accounts, as well as how much you owe on different types of accounts (credit card, auto loan, mortgages, and so on).

To put this in perspective: Most Americans use less than 30 percent of their available credit limits, according to Fair Isaac. Only one in six uses 80 percent or more of available limits.

As you might expect, using a much higher percentage of your limits will worry lenders and potentially hurt your score. People who max out their credit limits, or even come close, tend to have a much higher rate of default than people who keep their credit use under control.

When it comes to revolving debt—credit cards and lines of credit—the credit score formula looks at the difference between your credit limits on the accounts and your balance, or the amount of credit you're actually using. The bigger the gap between your balance and your limit, the better.

Here's a point that needs clarification: Lenders report your balances to the credit bureaus on a given day (usually each month, but sometimes only every other month or quarterly). It doesn't matter whether you pay the balance off in full the next day—the balance you owed on the reporting day is what shows up on your credit report. That's why people who pay off their credit cards in full every month still might have balances showing on their reports.

So you need to be careful with how much you charge, even if you never carry a balance from month to month. Your total balance during the month should never approach your credit limit if you want a good score.

The score also looks at how much you owe on installment loans (mortgages, auto loans) compared to what you originally borrowed. Paying down the balances over time tends to help your score.

How Long You've Had Credit

This is 15 percent of your total score. As such, it's generally much less important than the previous two factors, but it still matters. You can have a good score with a short history, but typically the longer you've had credit, the better.

To put this in perspective: The average American's oldest account has been established for about 18 years, according to Fair Isaac. One in three has an account that's been established for 20 years or more.

The score considers both of the following:

- The age of your oldest account

- The average age of all your accounts

Your Last Application for Credit

This is 10 percent of your overall score. Opening new accounts can ding your credit score, particularly if you apply for a lot of credit in a short time and you don't have a long credit history.

To put this in perspective: The average American has not opened an account in 15 months.

The score factors in the following:

- How many accounts you've applied for recently

- How many new accounts you've opened

- How much time has passed since you applied for credit

- How much time has passed since you opened an account

You might have heard that "shopping around" for credit can hurt your score. We deal with this issue more thoroughly in Chapter 4, "Improving Your Score—The Right Way," but the FICO formula takes into account that people tend to shop around for important loans such as mortgages and auto financing. As long as you do your shopping in a fairly concentrated period of time, it shouldn't affect the score used for your application.

Also, pulling your own credit report and score doesn't affect your score. As long as you do it yourself, ordering from a credit bureau or a reputable intermediary, the inquiry won't count against you. If you have a lender pull your score "just to see it," though, you could end up hurting your score.

The Types of Credit You Use

This is 10 percent of your score. The FICO scoring formula wants to see a "healthy mix" of credit, but Fair Isaac is customarily vague about what that means.

The company does say that you don't need to have a loan of each possible type—credit card, mortgage, auto loan, and so on—to have a good score. Furthermore, you're cautioned against applying for credit you don't need to boost your score because that can backfire.

To get the highest possible scores, however, you need to have both revolving debts like credit cards and installment debts like an auto loan, mortgage, or personal loan. These latter loans don't have to still be open to influence your score. But they do still need to show up on your credit report.

Bankcards—major credit cards such as Visa, MasterCard, American Express, Discover, and Diner's Club—are typically better for your credit score than department store or other "finance company" cards. (Department stores' cards are typically issued by finance companies, which specialize in consumer lending and which, unlike banks, don't receive deposits.)

Installment loans can reflect well on you, too. That's because lenders generally require more documentation and take a closer look at your credit before granting the loan.

To put this in perspective: The average American has 15 credit accounts showing on their credit report, including 9 credit cards and 6 installment loans, according to Fair Isaac.

Your Credit Scorecard

How these five factors are weighed when it comes to *you*—as opposed to the general population—depends on a little-known sorting system known at Fair Isaac as "scorecards."

Scorecards allow the FICO formula to segment borrowers into one of ten different groups, based on information in their credit reports.

If the credit history shows only positive information, the model takes into account the following:

- The number of accounts

- The age of the accounts

- The age of the youngest account

If the history shows a serious delinquency, the model looks for these:

- The presence of any public record, such as a bankruptcy or tax lien

- The worst delinquency, if there's more than one on the file

After the model has this information, it decides which of its scorecards to assign. Although Fair Isaac keeps many of the details secret, it's known that there is at least one scorecard for people with a bankruptcy in their backgrounds, and another for people who don't have much information in their reports. The FICO formula used by many mortgage lenders has 10 scorecards, with 2 reserved for people with significant credit problems, while a newer version of the formula known as FICO 8 has 12 scorecards with 4 that apply to people with serious credit negatives. With FICO 9, the number of scorecards has been increased to 13.

Grouping people this way is supposed to enhance the formula's predictive power. The theory is that the same behavior in different borrowers can mean different things. Someone with a troubled credit history who suddenly opens a slew of accounts, for example, might be seen as a much greater risk than someone with a long, clean history. Scorecards allow the FICO formula to give different weight to the same information.

Sometimes, however, the actual results of the scorecards can be a little bizarre.

Naomi of Richmond, Virginia, spent years rebuilding her credit and couldn't wait for the seven-year mark to pass on three negative items on her credit report: two collection actions and a judgment. These items, she was sure, were the only things holding her credit score down.

When the black marks disappeared from her report, however, Naomi's score actually *dropped* more than 20 points. Naomi got caught in what can be a jarring transition from one scorecard to the next.

The negative items on her credit report got her assigned to a certain scorecard, but her efforts to rebuild her credit—making payments on time and using credit responsibility—helped her rise to the top of that scorecard group.

When her negative marks disappeared, though, she was transferred to another group with tougher standards. In that group, she was closer to the bottom, and her credit score drop reflected her fall.

Naomi's only solace was that the responsible credit behavior she had learned would help boost her score and recover lost ground over time.

The latest versions of the FICO formula means that fewer people will see the big drops Naomi experienced, according to Fair Isaac. The company says more scorecards mean a smoother transition from one group to another as credit information changes.

Your Results Might Differ

You need to know about a few more complications.

Although all three bureaus use the FICO scoring model, the actual formulas differ slightly from bureau to bureau. That's because the way the bureaus collect and report data isn't exactly the same. It's unlikely that these differences would have much impact on your score, but you should know that they exist. You're much more likely, though, to have different scores from bureau to bureau because the underlying information is different.

As discussed earlier, lenders can have their own in-house scoring formulas in addition to, or instead of, using FICO scores. Lenders also can use different versions of the FICO formula. Just as not everyone updates to the latest computer operating systems when they're released, not every lender uses the latest versions of credit-scoring formulas customized to certain industries—such as auto loans and bankcards—and they can use different generations of the formulas.

Older versions of the FICO formula, for example, counted participation in a credit-counseling program as a negative factor; newer versions view it as a neutral factor. So, if you're currently in a debt management program, you might be viewed more negatively by some lenders than by others.

Just consider what happened to Marvin, a home buyer who learned too late that his scores weren't what he thought they were.

Marvin purchased scores from each of the three credit bureaus. Because lenders usually use the middle of your three scores to determine your interest rates, Marvin was happy to discover his middle score was 638—not great, but high enough to avoid the 620 mark many lenders used at the time to classify a borrower as subprime, or high risk.

When Marvin applied for a loan, however, the lender told him his middle score was 593. Marvin paid the price for the discrepancy:

> *"No one tells you this when you pay your money to get your score,"*
> *Marvin said. "We actually put our house on the market based*
> *on the information we received from the agencies, having to*
> *scramble later for a mortgage company to accept our lower score.*
> *We went from being able to receive competitive interest rates to*
> *being considered very high risk and receiving very high rates."*

You can help protect yourself somewhat from these discrepancies by being preapproved for a home loan before you start house shopping. But this is just another reason why it's important to improve and protect your score. The higher your score is, the less you have to worry about a few points making a difference.

How Do I Get My Score?

If you've surfed the Internet lately, you might find it hard to believe that credit scores were once considered secret. Sometimes it seems like every other Web site is either hawking credit scores or running an ad for a Web site that does.

As you've read, though, not all credit scores are created equal.

The credit bureaus, for example, sometimes market scores to consumers that aren't based on the FICO formula—the one typically used by lenders. The bureaus say these scores are a good indicator of a consumer's creditworthiness, but their results can differ—sometimes markedly—from the FICO numbers that lenders use. If the score you're looking at doesn't say FICO, it's not the same formula most lenders use.

Be careful not to be misled by pitches that promise "free" access to your credit score, and then require you to sign up for credit monitoring or other ongoing services that are most assuredly not free. Although you might decide that these services are helpful, make sure to read the fine print so that you understand what you're getting and how you can cancel if necessary. Another caution: Some fly-by-night operators might pitch credit scores as a way to get you to reveal your private financial information, such as your Social Security number or credit card numbers. As always on the Web, it's best to do business with companies you know and to make sure you have a secure connection before transmitting sensitive information. Congress in 2003 gave U.S. residents the right to get free copies of their credit reports annually from each of the three bureaus at a single site: www.annualcreditreport.com. But that doesn't include the right to free scores; the bureaus can and will continue to charge for those.

A growing number of credit card issuers and other outlets now offer customers regular access to at least one of their FICO scores. Discover, BarclayCard, and Chase Slate, among others, include a FICO score on customers' monthly statements as part of Fair Isaac's Open Access program. FICO scores also are available to many non-profit credit counseling agencies.

If you don't have access to a free FICO score, you can buy scores from MyFICO.com, a joint venture between Fair Isaac and Equifax. The site offers your credit reports and FICO scores (currently FICO 8) from all three major bureaus—Equifax, Experian, and TransUnion—for $19.95 each.

You don't get just a single score, however. After you buy one bureau score from MyFICO, the site shows you five or six other commonly used FICOs lenders buy from that bureau to evaluate you, such as mortgage, auto, and bankcard scores.

When I bought my scores recently, for example, my FICO 8 from Equifax was 846 on the 300-to-850 scale. But my FICO 5, the score Equifax most commonly sells to mortgage lenders, was 797. The first score was considered "exceptional," according to MyFICO, whereas the second was "very good."

There was even wider variation in my auto and credit card scores, which used a 250-to-900 scale. My FICO Auto Score 8 was 867, whereas my FICO Auto Score 5 was 810. My FICO Bankcard Score 8 was 869 and my FICO Bankcard Score 5 was 797.

My scores from Experian ranged from 796 (FICO Score 3, used by some credit card issuers) to 878 (FICO Auto Score 8). The clutch of numbers from TransUnion ran from 806 (FICO Score 4, used by some mortgage lenders) to 874 (FICO Auto Score 8).

Does the variation in scores concern me? Not at all, since I know any one of those scores is high enough to get a lender's best rate and terms. The fact that I could view 19 different scores from one company on a single day, though, helps to illustrate the wide range of numbers that can be used to evaluate borrowers.

Other helpful features of the MyFICO site include

- A simulator, which can help you see what could happen to your FICO 8 if you opened a new account, skipped a payment, filed for bankruptcy, or took other positive or negative actions

- A chart showing what rates you could expect on mortgages, home equity lines of credit, and car loans

In Figure 2.1, the borrower has an Experian FICO score of 776, which puts her ahead of about 73 percent of other Americans.

Figure 2.1 How you rank

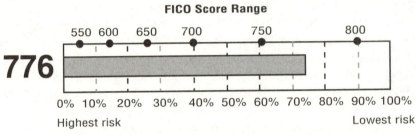

Source: Fair Isaac Co. Used by permission.

Because the primary purpose of a FICO score is to predict default risk, you might be interested to know how you stack up in that regard. As you can see from the chart in Figure 2.2, the risk of fault rises dramatically as scores drop.

Figure 2.2 Your risk of default

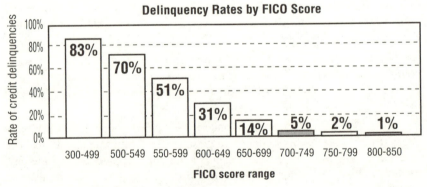

Source: Fair Isaac Co. Used by permission.

When you get a score from MyFICO.com, you'll get a summary of the major factors influencing your score. Be sure to read these carefully, along with any additional explanatory information. These factors are provided to give you some clues about how to improve your score, but if you misinterpret the results, you could end up making things worse.

For example, many people with good credit often think that one of the reasons their score isn't higher is that they have too many credit cards. They think they can solve the problem by closing cards, but the FICO formula doesn't work that way. For one thing, having several open and responsibly used credit accounts is typically good for your scores. For another, closed cards remain on your credit report and continue to influence your score. In fact, the act of closing accounts can actually hurt your score, as I explain later.

The positive factors you'll see should be listed in order of importance and might be something like the following:

- You have no late payments reported on your credit accounts.

- You demonstrate a relatively long credit history.

- You have a low proportion of balances to credit limits on your revolving/charge accounts.

Negative factors, too, should be listed in order of importance. If you have a bankruptcy, collections action, or other serious delinquency, that would be mentioned first. Other negatives that can show up for even the best borrowers include the following:

- You have recently been seeking credit or other services, as reflected by the number of inquiries posted on your credit file in the past 12 months.

- You have a relatively high number of consumer finance company accounts being reported.

- The proportion of balances to credit limits (high credit) on your revolving/charge accounts is too high.

- The length of time your accounts have been established is relatively short.

Now, nobody likes criticism, and some people get absolutely furious when they read through the reasons they're given for why their score isn't higher. Interestingly, many of these folks tend to have excellent credit, but—like Brian in the previous chapter—they're angry that their score isn't "perfect."

Understand that nobody is "perfect," and even if you could achieve a perfect FICO score, the changing circumstances of your life and your credit use would mean you wouldn't keep that score for long.

Also understand that the negative reasons listed are less and less important the higher your score. The bureaus need to give you some reason for why your scores aren't higher, but when your score is already in the mid-700s and above, there's no guarantee that even if you could fix the "problem" that your scores would rise that much.

Still, you can always learn something from reading the reasons given. A notation that your balances are too high should spur you to pay down your debt, for your own financial health as well as for the sake of your score. Getting dinged for opening too many cards should keep you from applying for yet another department store card just to get a 10 percent discount. You probably don't need one more piece of plastic to keep track of, anyway.

If your score is low, however, you should take the negative factors to heart. They can provide a blueprint for fixing your credit and boosting your score. In Chapter 4, you'll find general information about improving your score, and in later chapters, I discuss more specific strategies for people who have troubled credit.

What Hurts and for How Long

For a decade after revealing the basics of how FICOs work, Fair Isaac resisted telling us exactly how certain actions affected our scores and how long it would take those numbers to recover.

In recent years, though, the company has given us a much clearer idea of what we might face from common credit setbacks. The chart in Figure 2.3 shows how many points you could lose from late payments, a short sale, a foreclosure, and a bankruptcy, depending on your initial scores. If you had an initial FICO score of about 780, for example, you could lose up to 110 points from a single skipped mortgage payment and a whopping 240 points if you filed for bankruptcy. Someone with a mediocre 680 score would lose fewer points: up to 80 for a missed payment or 150 for a bankruptcy. It might not seem fair that someone with a worse score loses less, but remember: Credit scores aren't designed to be fair. They're designed to gauge your risk of default. Someone with a lower score already has a higher risk of default, so another negative mark is less of a surprise and trims less from her score.

Figure 2.3 How financial setbacks affect your FICOs

Impact to FICO Score	Consumer A	Consumer B	Consumer C
Starting FICO Score	~ 680	~ 720	~ 780
FICO Score after these events:			
30 days late on mortgage	600-620	630-650	670-690
90 days late on mortgage	600-620	610-630	650-670
Short sale / deed-in-lieu / settlement (no deficiency balance)	610-630	605-625	655-675
Short sale (with deficiency balance)	575-595	570-590	620-640
Foreclosure	575-595	570-590	620-640
Bankruptcy	530-550	525-545	540-560

Source: FICO® Banking Analytics Blog. © 2011 Fair Isaac Corporation.

People with lower scores also recover faster from credit setbacks because they don't have as far to go to return to their initial scores. The person who starts with a 680 score can get back to her original score within nine months after a skipped payment, whereas her friend with a 780 score would take about three years of error-free behavior to restore her higher score. The person with a 680 score would recover from a bankruptcy in about five years, whereas the 780 scorer would need seven to ten years—in other words, she might not recover fully until the bankruptcy dropped off her credit reports.

Figure 2.4 Estimated time for FICO score to fully recover

Estimated Time for FICO Score to Fully Recover	Consumer A	Consumer B	Consumer C
Starting FICO Score	~ 680	~ 720	~ 780
Time for FICO to recover:			
30 days late on mortgage	~ 9 months	~ 2.5 years	~ 3 years
90 days late on mortgage	~ 9 months	~ 3 years	~ 7 years
Short sale / deed-in-lieu / settlement (no deficiency balance)	~ 3 years	~ 7 years	~ 7 years
Short sale (with deficiency balance)	~ 3 years	~ 7 years	~ 7 years
Foreclosure	~ 3 years	~ 7 years	~ 7 years
Bankruptcy	~ 5 years	~ 7–10 years	~ 7–10 years

Note: Estimates assume all else held constant over time (for example, no new account openings, no new delinquency, similar outstanding debt).

Source: FICO® Banking Analytics Blog. © 2011 Fair Isaac Corporation.

One other thing you should note from these charts: Short sales and foreclosures can have the same impact on your scores. Short sales are when your lender agrees to let you sell your home for less than what you owe. The way these transactions are reported by the lender to the credit bureaus, though, can vary. Early in the last recession, lenders typically reported short sales using the code for a settlement and reported the deficiency balance—the difference between what you owe and the sale price—to the credit bureaus. The impact was much the same as a foreclosure. As the number of short sales piled up, though, many lenders began to report them in less damaging ways.

In whatever way a short sale is reported, though, it's typically treated more favorably by mortgage lenders than a foreclosure. Many lenders will consider your application for another mortgage after two years have passed since the short sale, whereas you may have to wait up to seven years after a foreclosure.

New Versions of the FICO Score

Although mortgage lenders typically use an older version of the score, other lenders have flocked to the FICO 8, which was launched in 2008. Fair Isaac promised FICO 8 would do a better job of predicting defaults, particularly among customers with poor, thin, or young credit histories. Compared to the FICO used by most mortgage lenders, FICO 8:

- Is less punishing to those who have had a serious credit set-back, such as a charge-off or a repossession, as long as their other active credit accounts are all in good standing.

- Entirely ignores small collections where the original debt was less than $100. (This is a huge victory for consumers, many of whose credit reports have been tarnished by small-ticket disputes and minor medical bills their insurance companies failed to pay.)

- Is even more sensitive to the balances reported on consumers' credit cards.

- Responds more positively if borrowers have both revolving and installment accounts.

- Responds more negatively if consumers have few open, active accounts.

- Protects against so-called authorized user abuse.

As I discuss in Chapter 4, adding a spouse or child to your credit card as an authorized user has long been a good way to boost that person's credit score because your good history with the account could be imported to his credit file. But in 2007, credit repair firms began abusing this feature by "renting" authorized user slots from good credit risks and selling them to complete strangers who wanted to boost their scores. Some of these strangers bought slots on dozens of different people's cards, boosting their scores by tens or even hundreds of points.

Fair Isaac originally said FICO 8 would combat possible fraud by ignoring all authorized user information, drawing protests from consumer advocates who pointed out that the change would punish the innocent as well as the guilty. Furthermore, experts theorized that ignoring information regarding spouses on authorized credit lines could be a violation of the Equal Credit Opportunity Act.

So Fair Isaac rejiggered the FICO 8 formula to include authorized user accounts "while materially reducing potential impacts to the score," according to the company's FICO 8 marketing brochure. Exactly how it does that is as secret as the rest of the formula, but speculation is that the score counts a limited number of authorized user accounts and ignores the rest.

Fair Isaac also built a score for the mortgage lenders based on this model. For the FICO Mortgage Score, the company's scientists fine-tuned the FICO 8 formula to be more sensitive to the possibility of mortgage defaults. As of this writing, however, the FICO Mortgage Score has yet to receive the blessing of Fannie Mae and Freddie Mac, so home lenders have stuck to the older versions.

Outside the mortgage industry, though, FICO 8 is a hit. It is now the most commonly used credit score, according to Fair Isaac. Fortunately, all the strategies I outline in Chapter 4 for improving your score work with both iterations of the FICO score.

FICO 8 isn't the last word in credit scores, of course. In 2015, Fair Isaac launched FICO 9. The new score completely ignores paid collections and treats medical collections as less severe than other types of collections.

This latter change reflects a fairly sharp turnabout by Fair Isaac. In the past, consumer advocates had decried the effect medical bills could have on people's credit. People who were responsible with their credit cards and loans still could face overwhelming medical bills because they didn't have health insurance, or the coverage they had wasn't adequate. Even those who were adequately insured could be vulnerable to credit score downgrades when the convoluted insurance reimbursement system allowed bills to fall through the cracks.

For years, Fair Isaac rejected those arguments, saying its research didn't support separating medical from other collections. In 2014, the federal Consumer Finance Protection Bureau called that into question with a study that found medical collections weren't as predictive of future defaults as other collections. Eventually, Fair Isaac reached the same conclusion.

It's still too early to tell how quickly lenders will adopt the latest scoring system. Because you're most likely to face one of the earlier scores, read the following scenarios Fair Isaac created to demonstrate how FICO 8 works compared to the FICO used in the mortgage industry.

FICO 8 Score: Three Consumer Scenarios

Scenario 1: Higher-risk consumers

Consider two people named Jose and Alicia who have similar credit histories:

- Each has about ten accounts (open or closed) on their credit report.

- Each has been managing credit for about ten years based on the age of their oldest reported accounts.

- Each has at least one major account delinquency on their credit report (such as a charge-off or repossession).

- Neither has a public record on their credit report (such as a tax lien or bankruptcy).

- Each has a previous-generation FICO credit score of about 625.

When a lender checks their FICO 8 scores, however, Alicia receives a score of about 650, whereas Jose receives a score of about 600. Here's what led to this difference in outcomes.

Alicia receives a FICO 8 score of 650:

- Compared to Jose, Alicia's credit report shows a relatively higher number of open accounts that are reported as paid-as-agreed. So she received more points for having credit accounts in good standing.

- Her credit report demonstrates she has had a mixture of revolving (credit cards) and installment (auto loan, student loan, and so on) accounts. So she received more points for demonstrating a good ability to handle a variety of credit types.

Jose receives a FICO 8 score of 600:

- Compared to Alicia, Jose's credit report shows more closed accounts and fewer open accounts that are reported as paid-as-agreed. So his score is lower in response to his report showing that he has comparatively less recent experience in managing credit responsibly.

- His credit report also has no open or active install-ment loan account on file. So his score is lower due to a lack of demonstration that he has successfully man-aged a variety of credit types.

Scenario 2: Thin-file consumers

Now consider two consumers named Bill and Jennifer who have similar credit histories:

- They each established their first credit account less than three years ago.
- They each now have five accounts listed on their cred-it report.
- Neither credit report shows a serious credit delinquen-cy (90 days or more past due).
- Each has a previous-generation FICO credit score of about 665.

When a lender checks their FICO 8 scores, Bill receives a score of about 685, whereas Jennifer receives a score of about 645. Here's what led to this difference in outcomes.

Bill receives a FICO 8 score of 685:

- His credit report shows that he has a relatively larger number of open accounts that have been paid-as-agreed.
- None of his reported accounts has a high balance relative to the credit limit.

Jennifer receives a FICO 8 score of 645:

- Her credit report shows that she has relatively few active, open accounts compared to Bill. This means there is less evidence in her file that she is handling her credit well.
- She has at least one revolving account with a high balance relative to the credit limit. This is significant in her case because higher credit utilization can have greater weight as a risk factor in the calculation of FICO 8 scores.

Scenario 3: Mainstream consumers

Now consider two more consumers named Isabel and Fred who have similar credit histories:

- The oldest account on their respective credit reports is about ten years old.
- Their credit reports each contain between 15 and 20 accounts.
- Neither credit report shows a serious credit delinquency (90 days or more past due).
- Each has a previous-generation FICO credit score of about 725.

When a lender checks their FICO 8 scores, Isabel receives a score of about 745, whereas Fred receives a score of about 705. Here's what led to this difference in outcomes.

Isabel receives a FICO 8 score of 745:

- Compared to Fred, Isabel has lower balances and is using comparatively less of her available credit. She also has more credit card accounts on her credit report that show a balance. Combined, these two factors demonstrate that she is actively using her credit and is handling it responsibly.
- Her credit report also contains an open auto loan account that has mostly been paid off. So she received more points for demonstrating a good ability to handle a variety of credit types.

Fred receives a FICO 8 score of 705:

- Compared to Isabel, Fred's report shows more credit card accounts with higher balances. Because having high utilization correlates to statistically greater credit risk, it lowers his score.
- While he has an open auto loan on his credit report, very little has been paid down from the original loan amount. So although Fred's score benefits from the variety of credit types on his report, he hasn't yet demonstrated the ability to handle installment loans over time, and this is reflected in his receiving fewer points in this area than Isabel.

3

VantageScore—A FICO Rival Emerges

I regularly hear from readers who thought they knew what their credit scores were—until they applied for a loan and found their lenders used dramatically different numbers. These readers are often astonished, and outraged, to learn that the credit scores they bought aren't the ones lenders use. Consumer advocates complained that the "consumer education scores" sold by credit bureaus and other sources could be 30 points, or more, higher than comparable FICO scores.

This situation led some to label these alternative scores as "FAKO" scores, with the clear implication that the sellers are trying to deceive people with fake merchandise. That might not be quite fair, but the bureaus' repeated insistence that "a credit score is a credit score," and that it doesn't matter which one you get, is disingenuous.

It's true that the FICO scores you get from MyFICO.com might not be exactly the same as the FICO scores your lenders pull, because lenders use different versions of the FICO and those versions can be tweaked for different industries. But at least you'll be in the right ballpark.

If you're getting one of these alternative scores for free, it might not matter to you that you're not seeing an actual FICO. If you're paying for the score, though, you should make sure you're getting what you expect. If it doesn't say it's a FICO, it's not a FICO.

There is another scoring formula, though, that's gaining ground with lenders *and* consumers: the VantageScore.

The three major credit bureaus—Experian, Equifax, and TransUnion—made a big splash in March 2006 when they announced this new credit-scoring system. In an unprecedented move, the three competing bureaus worked together to create a scoring system to rival the entrenched FICO.

Using words such as *innovative, consistent,* and *accurate,* the bureaus strongly implied that they had created a better mousetrap.

Many media outlets picked up the hype, proclaiming that VantageScores were an improvement on the FICO scores that most lenders use. Articles and broadcasts proclaimed the new credit score was "great news for consumers," that it would "simplify" or "remake" the credit application process. One columnist even proclaimed, with little apparent evidence, that "creditworthy people...are more likely to get credit now."

People who know about credit scoring took a decidedly more "wait and see" attitude. So far, VantageScore has not managed to push FICO off its perch as the leading credit score. But unlike other competitors, VantageScore has gained at least a toehold in the credit scoring market. The bureaus announced in 2015 that the formula was being used for at least some lending decisions by 2,000 lenders, including 6 of the 10 largest banks, and that nearly 1 billion VantageScores had been pulled so far.

Even more important, an additional 3 billion scores had been pulled for modeling and testing purposes—indicating many more lenders are in the process of adopting the formula. All the activity indicates that VantageScore has become a solid competitor to the venerable FICO score.

Furthermore, VantageScore has made arrangements with several consumer sites to offer its scores for free, including CreditKarma, CreditSesame, Credit.com, and Quizzle, among others. And VantageScore revised the language for its reason codes, which explain what's affecting a score, to make them more understandable to the average person. All this outreach has helped boost VantageScore's profile.

The VantageScore Scale

Initially, the VantageScore used a totally different scale from the FICO: VantageScores ran from 501 to 990. To make the score more "intuitive," the bureaus designed each tier to correspond to the alphabetic grading system that most of us know from elementary school:

901–990 equals A credit

801–900 equals B credit

701–800 equals C credit

601–700 equals D credit

501–600 equals F credit

At the time the bureaus announced the VantageScore, they released statistics showing the percentage of population with each "grade." Put those statistics next to similar statistics supplied by Fair Isaac for FICO scores, and you'll soon notice something interesting.

VantageScore	% with Score	FICO Score	% with Score
900–990 A	11%	800–850	13%
801–900 B	29%	750–799	27%
701–800 C	21%	700–749	18%
601–700 D	20%	650–699	15%
501–600 F	19%	600–649	12%
		550–599	8%
		500–549	5%
		300–499	2%

The two scoring systems manage to put similar percentages of people in their highest three tiers. The FICO scale offers more tiers at the lower end than VantageScore, but the percentage of folks in the basement appears roughly the same.

Under the VantageScore system, 19 percent of borrowers at the time had F credit. If you use a FICO score of 620 as a cutoff point for subprime credit, you get similar results: Fair Isaac said that 19 percent of consumers had FICO scores below 620.

The bureaus and Fair Isaac cautioned against drawing conclusions from this comparison about where any consumer might stand in one system versus the other. But people did, and some wondered why a 750 score would be considered very good in one system and mediocre in another.

Consumer confusion wasn't the only downside of VantageScore's 500-to-990 scale. Lenders had built their software systems around FICO's 300-to-850 scale, and they weren't eager to make the changes needed to accept a different scale. Even FICO, with its ill-fated NextGen score, failed to persuade its customers that it was worth the effort. So perhaps it's not surprising that VantageScore eventually switched to the 300-to-850 scale with its latest version, 3.0.

VantageScore 3.0 made a few other important changes. It stopped counting paid collections, saying they weren't predictive of future default. It also looked back farther into the credit histories of people who hadn't recently used credit. As you've read, FICO requires at least one account to be updated within the previous six months. VantageScore looks back 24 months. Finally, VantageScore can generate a score for someone whose credit is just 30 days old. FICO requires that people have one account that's at least six months old. Those last two features mean as many as 35 million more people can be scored with VantageScores.

How VantageScores Are Calculated

Like FICO scores, VantageScores are calculated using the information in your credit reports. The factors considered are similar—your payment history, your balances, your credit limits, how long you've had credit, how recently you've applied for credit, and the mix of credit accounts in your file.

Exactly how each of these factors was weighted has changed over time as the score evolved (see Figure 3.1). Initially, for example, "recent credit activities" made up about 10 percent of VantageScore 1.0. In the second version, that was bumped up to 30 percent. In 3.0, it was demoted back to a "less influential" factor, comprising 5 percent of the score.

Figure 3.1   VantageScore weightings have changed over time

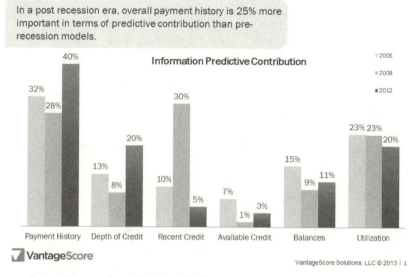

In a post recession era, overall payment history is 25% more important in terms of predictive contribution than pre-recession models.

Information Predictive Contribution

- 2005
- 2009
- 2012

Payment History — 32%, 28%, 40%
Depth of Credit — 13%, 8%, 20%
Recent Credit — 10%, 30%, 5%
Available Credit — 7%, 1%, 3%
Balances — 15%, 9%, 11%
Utilization — 23%, 23%, 20%

VantageScore

VantageScore Solutions, LLC © 2013 | 1

Source: VantageScore Solutions LLC.

Which leads us to another change. VantageScore Solutions, the company that offers the formula, is trying to move away from the "35 percent is this, 30 percent is that" explainer that proved so helpful to understanding FICO scores. VantageScore says those "pie charts" are misleading because what might heavily influence one person's score might be less relevant to another's.

So now the company mostly talks about how influential factors are. Your payment history—essentially, paying bills on time—is "extremely influential." Age and type of credit, and credit utilization, are "highly influential." "Moderately influential" are the total balances you owe. Recent credit behavior and inquiries, and available credit, are "less influential" factors.

This means at least some of the basic rules are the same between the systems. Here's how to protect and improve your score:

- Pay bills on time.

- Pay down your debt.

- Don't open too many new accounts too quickly.

So Which Is Better?

The bureaus say they built VantageScore from the ground up, using their own expertise and databases. When announcing the new scoring system, the bureaus were careful not to compare it directly to the FICO score. In fact, when asked, bureau spokespeople continue to say that the VantageScore formula hadn't been tested head to head with the FICO.

What VantageScore says to lenders is that its 3.0 score is more predictive than unspecified "benchmarks," and that it does a better job of predicting which prime and near-prime consumers will default.

VantageScore's Future

When VantageScore was announced, many credit experts predicted the new system would have a tough time unseating the classic FICO score. That assessment appears to have been correct, but the score is doing better than some expected.

Changing to a FICO-style scale doubtless helped. The scale is deeply embedded in the complex, highly automated formulas that lenders use to evaluate current and potential borrowers. Switching to a new range can be expensive and difficult. Credit expert John Ulzheimer, who has worked for both Equifax and Fair Isaac, put it this way: "It's kind of like spending $10,000 to replace a $1 part, and the $1 part isn't even broken."

VantageScore also made strides in getting its score accepted for the process that Wall Street calls *securitization*, in which loans are bundled up and sold to investors. FICO scores have long been used to evaluate and price these investments, but now VantageScores are sometimes used as well.

One nut VantageScore has yet to crack is the same one that FICO has struggled with: getting major mortgage buyers Fannie Mae and Freddie Mac to accept a new score. Most mortgage loans are made under the guidance of these two "government-sponsored enterprises," and that guidance has specified that lenders use a version of the FICO that's now several generations out of date.

The wheels of government certainly turn slowly, but VantageScore still hopes those wheels will soon turn in its favor. Other regulators have accepted the score, the company says, so it may be just a matter of time before the mortgage industry catches up.

Of course, the bureaus have a strong incentive to win over lenders and rating agencies: money.

Every time a bureau generates a FICO score for a lender, the bureau has to pay a fee to Fair Isaac. It's a profitable business for the company: According to Merrill Lynch analyst Edward Maguire, credit scoring at one point accounted for 20 percent of Fair Isaac's revenues but 65 percent of its operating profits.

By creating and selling their own scoring system, the bureaus cut out the middleman.

The bureaus individually have tried to break Fair Isaac's grip on the credit-scoring market before without much success. They're hoping this joint effort—which promises a FICO-like consistent scoring formula across all three bureaus—will win over lenders who were reluctant to buy bureaus' previous efforts to create proprietary scores.

A side note here: In unveiling the VantageScore, the bureaus made a big deal about its consistency. They touted the fact that their formula could take into account the different ways that the bureaus reported various bits of credit information and deliver scores that were consistent and comparable across all three agencies.

That caused some in the media to conclude that the FICO methodology is somehow different at each bureau. In fact, consistency has long been FICO's trademark. It, too, uses the same formula across all three bureaus, with minor tweaks designed to accommodate the reporting differences at each agency.

Most of the variation in consumers' scores among the three bureaus is caused by differences in the underlying data. You might have accounts reported at one bureau that don't show up at the other two, or you might have successfully disputed an error at two of the bureaus that still shows up at the third. Neither the FICO nor the VantageScore fixes that problem; it's still the information on each bureau's credit report—accurate or not—that's used to calculate the scores.

Other Scores Lenders Use

Credit scores aren't the only scores—or even the most commonly used scores—lenders use to judge you.

Your credit card issuer checks your credit scores when you apply for credit and perhaps once a month after that. But your issuer also consults other scores, some of which are generated every time you use your card. The most commonly created score is a transaction score, designed to flag whether the purchase being made might be fraudulent. Other scores help determine

- The kind of credit card offers you get

- Whether your credit limits are raised or suddenly lowered

- Whether your card issuer calls you about a suspicious transaction, blocks it, or shuts down your account

- How cooperative your issuer is about waiving fees or lowering your interest rate

- How quickly your issuer calls you if your payment is late

- Whether a collection agency contacts you about an old debt and how hard it pushes

Here are some of the scores and what they're designed to do:

- **Application score**—This score factors in data from your credit application that's not included in your credit scores, such as your income, how long you've lived at your current address, and how long you've worked for your current employer. Lenders usually use application scores with other scores, such as credit and bankruptcy scores, to decide whether to grant you credit, how much credit to extend, and what rate to charge.

- **Attrition-risk score**—Lenders don't want to lose their best customers, so they use attrition risk scores to try to figure out how likely you are to bolt to a competitor. Again, this score is used in combination with others to help the lender decide what to do next. If your account is profitable and you're seen as a low risk for default or bankruptcy, the company might try to win you back by lowering your rate, boosting your limit, or deluging you with convenience checks. If your attrition risk is high but so is your risk of default, the issuer might just let you go.

- **Bankruptcy score**—Credit scores typically predict the chance you'll miss a payment in the next two years. Bankruptcy scores predict the likelihood you'll stop paying entirely and seek to legally erase your debt. Most lenders use both to help assess the risk that you won't pay.

- **Behavior score**—Credit scores provide a broad overview of how you're handling all your various credit obligations. Behavior scores, by contrast, focus on how you handle a single account with the creditor who's calculating the score. Do you pay off your balances every month, carry a balance occasionally, or frequently pay only the minimum? That's not information that can be gleaned from a credit report, but the creditor can find this data in its own files. Lenders often use behavior scores along with credit and bankruptcy scores to decide whether, for example, an overdue payment is an unintentional lapse (maybe you're traveling) or a sign that you're in serious trouble.

- **Response score**—Only a tiny fraction of the credit card offers sent out in the mail generate an application. Lenders use response scores to try to boost that tiny fraction a tiny, profitable bit more. Response scores predict the likelihood a consumer will respond to an offer of credit, such as a new card or a balance transfer offer. Credit card issuers use response scores to decide whom to target and how to customize offers to appeal to particular consumers.

- **Revenue score**—It's all about the money, and revenue scores help lenders guess how much money—in interest payments, fees paid by the accountholder, and fees paid by merchants—an account is likely to generate.

- **Transaction score**—This is the score that's run every time you use a credit (or for that matter debit) card. Transaction scores compare the potential purchase to your previous buying activity, as well as to known patterns of fraud. A small purchase followed by a much larger one can be one red flag because fraudsters often "test" a card with a small purchase to make sure it's active before using the card to buy high-priced items that can be fenced. The rate of "false positives" for transaction scores is high; 20 purchases might be red-flagged for every one that's truly bogus. It's up to the issuer to decide where to set the bar that triggers account suspensions or review. Set it too high and the issuer can lose too much money, but setting it too low can aggravate customers by abruptly shutting down their accounts.

- **Collection score**—The scoring doesn't stop after you've defaulted on a debt. Collection agencies look for signs that you might be able or ready to pay, and collection scores can help them sort their list of debtors so the most likely prospects float to the top. The scores look for a variety of evidence that your financial situation may be improving, from better credit scores to another collector's account suddenly being paid.

Unlike credit scores, these other algorithms are used entirely in the background—you're unlikely to ever see the numbers being generated, and you have no legal right to request them. But they're being generated all the same.

4

Improving Your Score—
The Right Way

Okay, now you know your score, and you have a good idea of what goes into creating it. So, how do you make it better?

Step 1: Start with Your Credit Report

Because your credit score is based on your credit report, you should begin by ordering your reports from all three credit bureaus and reviewing each one for accuracy.

By federal law, U.S. consumers are entitled to one free credit report from each of the bureaus every year. You can order your reports from the Annual Credit Report Request Service by calling 877-322-8228 or by using its Web site, www.annualcreditreport.com. (If you use the online service, be sure to enter the Web site address correctly. If you mistype even one letter, you could wind up at the wrong site. In fact, be careful when entering "free credit report" or even "annualcreditreport.com" into a search engine, as sometimes the first results will be from lookalike sites trying to pass themselves off as the federal site.)

After you've used your free annual peeks, you can get additional reports from a service such as MyFico.com, or you can order from each bureau separately online or by phone:

- **Equifax**—www.equifax.com, 800-685-1111

- **Experian**—www.experian.com, 888-397-3742

- **TransUnion**—www.transunion.com, 800-916-8800

Canadians can also get their credit reports online:

- **Equifax Canada**—www.consumer.equifax.ca, 800-465-7166

- **TransUnion Canada**—www.tuc.ca, 800-663-9980

If you're accessing your reports online, you might want to print out the files to make the review process easier. At the very least, grab some paper and a pen to make a list of the changes needed as you go through the reports.

Exactly how your information is organized varies from report to report. But the basic sections are pretty similar and proceed more or less in the order outlined in this chapter.

Check the Identifying Information

At the top of each report is identifying information about you. Watch especially for the following:

- Names that aren't yours (not just misspellings of your own name)

- Social Security numbers that don't belong to you

- An incorrect birth date

- Addresses where you have never lived

These are the kinds of errors that could indicate someone else's information is in your file.

You might find other errors, such as an employer listed that you no longer work for or a misspelled address. You can ask the bureau to fix those problems as well, but that shouldn't be your highest priority.

Carefully Review the Credit Accounts

The next section lists credit accounts that you've opened, along with such information as the date you opened them, whether the account is still open or now closed, the type of account, the account number (typically abbreviated), your payment history, your credit limits, and your balances.

Scan this section closely for the following:

- Accounts that aren't yours

- Delinquencies that aren't yours (including late payments and charge-offs)

- Late payments, charge-offs, or other negative entries—other than a bankruptcy—that are more than seven years old

- Debts that your spouse incurred before marriage (unless they improve your credit history—more on that later)

- Any other incorrect account notations, such as showing a debt as past due when it was wiped out in a bankruptcy filing

If you find a number of incorrect entries, especially if they're delinquent or unpaid accounts, you could be a victim of identity theft. You'll find more information about how to handle this situation in Chapter 8, "Identity Theft and Your Credit."

On the other hand, you could be suffering from a credit bureau mix-up that accidentally merged someone else's information with yours. Although the bureaus say they have improved their systems to reduce the chances of this happening, it still occurs. I hear about it most often when two family members share similar names.

Don B. and his father have the same first and last names and share a middle initial. They live in different states (Florida and Indiana, respectively) and, of course, have different Social Security numbers. That hasn't prevented the credit bureaus from getting the two men confused.

When Don bought a piece of property recently, the bank pulled his credit reports from all three bureaus. He discovered that his and his father's credit information had been mixed together:

"For example, his car payment is on my report, but my car payment does not show up on my own report," Don said. "I was shocked at the number of discrepancies I found on each of the reports. As important as one's credit history is, one would think that these agencies would take the necessary steps to ensure accuracy."

You might find other errors, such as accounts you've long since closed still being reported as open, or not indicating accurately that you—rather than the creditor—closed the account.

The FICO scoring system doesn't really care who closes accounts, so you needn't worry too much about fixing those notations. And don't rush to change the notation on your closed accounts if they're listed as active; as I explain later, they could be helping your credit score.

Parse Through Your Inquiries

Inquiries show who has asked to review your credit report. Your credit score doesn't count inquiries made by lenders looking to make preapproved credit offers or your own requests to see your credit history. These are known as *soft* inquiries.

The inquiries that matter are the ones from lenders that resulted from you applying for credit. These are called *hard* inquiries.

What you do want to look for are these:

- Credit inquiries older than two years

- Hard credit inquiries that you didn't authorize

Add these to your list of items to dispute with the credit bureaus.

Examine Your Collections and Public Records

The final section of your credit report includes any collection actions or public records, including bankruptcies, foreclosures, garnishments, lawsuit judgments, and tax liens. Here's what you want to look for:

- Bankruptcies that are older than ten years or that aren't listed by the specific bankruptcy code chapter (Chapter 7, Chapter 13, and so on).

- Lawsuits, judgments, or paid tax liens older than seven years.

- Paid liens or judgments that are listed as unpaid.

- Duplicate collections, such as a loan that's listed under more than one collection agency. (An account you didn't pay often is listed twice, once with the original creditor and once with a collection agency, but there shouldn't be more than one collector listed at a time for the same debt.)

- Any negative information that isn't yours.

If in this review process you didn't find errors of note, skip to the next step. If you did, read on.

Dispute the Errors

Your credit report comes with a form for disputing errors by mail (if you ordered by phone) or online, depending on the way you ordered your report.

Credit bureaus are required by law to investigate any mistakes you bring to their attention and report back to you within 30 days. Typically they ask the creditor that reported the information to check its records. If the creditor can't vouch for the accuracy of what it reported or doesn't respond, the offending item is supposed to be deleted from your report.

The "investigation" process in the past hasn't been exactly robust. Complaints are often sent to subcontractors overseas, who determine a one- to three-digit code to summarize the problem before sending the dispute on to the creditor. The creditor may do nothing more than check its records to make sure the disputed information matches what was reported, without delving into its accuracy. Consumer advocates have long complained these investigations are far too perfunctory, leaving many people frustrated.

Problems could take months to resolve, if not longer. Even when people succeed in getting an error removed, it sometimes would simply reappear the next time the creditor uploaded information to the bureau.

Here's how a *New York Times* article summarized the situation:

"Because of these problems, credit-reporting bureaus have been sued repeatedly by regulators and consumers and have paid millions in fines and settlements. And yet the inaccuracies continue, consumers and their lawyers say, making them wonder if these companies view the penalties they pay as simply a cost of doing business."

In 2015, the bureaus finally promised to improve this investigation process. In a settlement with New York's attorney general, the bureaus said they would start using specially trained employees to deal with lingering disputes. In a second settlement with 31 state attorneys general, the bureaus also promised to create a process for handling complicated disputes, such as those involving identity theft, fraud, or mixed files, and to report to states the names of the lenders that made the most mistakes.

These changes could help people like Stan, a homeowner who encountered problems when his mortgage was transferred during a bank merger. The new bank made a mistake and reported to the credit bureaus that he was late with a $232 payment.

When Stan discovered the negative mark on his report, he contacted the bank and a representative agreed to fix the problem.

"She worked with me by giving me a letter stating [that the late payment was] reported in error," Stan said. Several months later, the late payment showed up again on his credit report. Stan contacted another bank official, who again promised to fix it after Stan faxed him the first representative's letter. When Stan pulled his report 60 days later, however, the delinquency was still there.

As you can see, the creditor holds a lot of power in this process. Although many errors are fixed promptly, permanently, and without fuss, an unethical or indifferent creditor could make your life difficult by verifying to the credit bureau that incorrect information is, in fact, accurate or simply re-reporting an old error. If you run into this problem, check out the information in "What to Do if the Credit Bureau Won't Budge" in Chapter 8.

If you're successful in getting errors removed from your report, you might—or might not—notice an improvement in your credit score. It all depends on the information remaining. The following section presents the best and most effective ways to make sure that information reflects well on you—and in your score.

Step 2: Pay Your Bills on Time

If you're new to the idea of credit scoring, you might have no idea how damaging just one late payment can be. I got this email from Brenda, a woman in Douglasville, Georgia, who was flabbergasted that all of her recent efforts to improve her credit score could be undone by one unpaid bill:

> *"I recently had a score of 640. I was late on a payment for a personal loan, and now it's 555. I now know that I can't afford to be late again, but that shouldn't have dropped my score that much, should it?"*

The truth is that one slip can erase years of good behavior. And the better your credit, the more a late payment can hurt.

Lenders are looking for any sign that you might default, and a late payment is often a good indicator that you're in financial trouble.

Because payment history makes up more than a third of the typical credit score, ensuring that your bills get paid on time—*all* the time—is essential.

Now, for those of you panicking over that credit card bill you sent in two days past the due date: You can stop sweating. Normally a payment has to be at least 30 days overdue for a creditor to report it to the bureaus.

That doesn't mean paying even a day late is a good idea, of course. Creditors are eager to slap their customers with late fees and can jack up interest rates on new balances in response to late payments.

You also can't skate on creditors that don't regularly report to credit bureaus. You might not have seen your cell phone account or your electric bill showing on your credit history, but that doesn't mean these vendors won't report your delinquencies if you don't pay them on time.

How to Make Sure Your Bills Get Paid on Time, All the Time

I occasionally get letters like the following, which try to put the blame for late payments on someone else:

> *"I recently checked my credit report after moving and found that my credit card company was reporting that I was 60 days overdue. I'm absolutely certain I haven't received the bill for that card in several months, or I would have paid it. Aren't they required to give me some notice before they report information like that to the credit bureaus?"*

This might be a shock to some folks, but the answer is no. *You're responsible for paying your bills whether you get a statement or not.* You need to keep track of what you owe to whom and make sure that everyone gets paid, even if the U.S. Postal Service falls down on the job.

Keeping track of these details also can help you detect identity theft. Some criminals like to steal credit card statements out of residential mailboxes. The bolder ones file a change-of-address form with the post office so that your mail gets redirected, allowing the bad guys to sort through it at their leisure.

To stay on top of what you owe and when, you should make a list of every bill you must pay each month and the date that it's due. Then list any bills that are due less regularly—every other month, every quarter, every six months, and annually.

Now, enter all your bills in your calendar. Get in the habit of checking that calendar at least weekly to see what bills are coming up and to make sure they're all getting paid.

You can set up electronic reminders to help you, as well:

- If you have a smartphone, you can configure its calendar to alert you.

- Many banks, credit cards, and online bill-pay systems offer free email or text reminder services.

- Bill-reminder features are part of personal finance software such as Quicken and online sites such as Mint.com.

If you really want to protect your credit, though, you should take further steps to avoid human error. The more of your bills that you pay automatically, the fewer worries you'll have about late payments, late charges, and dings on your bill.

There are a few options.

Automatic Debit

An automatic debit allows the companies that you owe to take their payments directly from your checking account each month, with no action on your part—no checkbook, no stamps, no fuss.

A lot of people balk at the idea of letting a mortgage lender, utility company, or other vendor have regular access to their bank accounts. Some feel it's somehow an invasion of privacy. In reality, the vendor can't "see" into your account or monitor what other activity is going on there. The money comes out basically the same way it would if you paid by check or by other electronic transfer.

A federal law prohibits vendors from taking out more than you authorize. If a mistake is made—and in more than two decades of paying bills automatically, it's only happened to me once, long ago—the company is obliged to replace the money it took in error.

Many people insist that they need control over when bills get paid. Typically, these folks have gotten into the bad habit of juggling bills or of not keeping enough cash in their checking account to cover their ongoing obligations. It's a good idea to always keep a "pad" of at least $100 in your checking account, regardless of how you pay your bills, and to sign up for true overdraft protection on your checking account. (True overdraft protection is tied to a line of credit or a savings account. It's not the same as the "bounce protection" banks infamously foisted on their customers—charging per-transaction fees of $30 or more and collecting billions—until Congress got involved.) Real overdraft protection, which usually costs less than $50 a year, can pay for itself the first couple of times you avoid a bounced check.

Or perhaps you've fallen into another bad habit—not paying your credit card balances in full. If that's the case, be sure to read later about how that can hurt your credit score. In the meantime, know that most credit card companies have several automatic payment options. They can take out just the minimum payment or a set dollar amount each month instead of the full statement balance. If you opt for these partial payments, you can always pay more by check or online.

Really, you only have two choices: to pay your bills on time, or pay them late. If you want good credit and don't want to worry about missing due dates, some kind of automatic payments is the answer for many, if not most, of your obligations. You will still get a bill each month with plenty of time to correct any problems on the statement before the payment is made.

You can start with a mortgage payment or a student loan because these payments tend to be the same each month, and the lenders might even give you a break on the rate if you agree to automatic debit. Just phone your lender or look online to see whether it offers this option. (Some call it "direct debit" or "direct payment.") Follow the lender's instructions, and your automatic payment typically will begin in a month or two.

You may not want to use automatic debit for everything, however. Certain vendors—health clubs, phone companies, and Internet service providers among them—are notorious for abusing automatic payment privileges by continuing to bill a customer after services have been discontinued. With these companies, it's probably best to use one of the methods discussed in the following sections.

Recurring Credit Card Charges

If you don't want to let vendors have access to your checking account, you can have many of your bills charged automatically on your credit card.

Using a credit card can give you an extra layer of protection because if a mistake is made, you have the credit card company to act as a middleman. You can dispute an erroneous charge and not have to pay it until the problem is resolved.

If you're using a rewards card, you also can get cash back, frequent flier miles, or other rewards points just for paying bills.

This method comes with two rather large caveats, though:

- **You should try this only if you can pay off the card in full each month**—Paying credit card interest is rarely a good idea, but it's never advised when you're paying basic monthly expenses.

- **Make sure your bills don't chew up too much of your available credit**—If paying your bills would bring you anywhere close to your credit limit, you'll be hurting—not helping—your score.

Online Bill Payment

Millions of people pay at least some of their bills online. Most credit cards, for example, allow you to log on and pay your balance from their sites. The most efficient online bill-pay systems, however, allow you to pay a variety of your bills from one Internet location—usually your bank's.

You can set up your system so that you decide when each bill gets paid, but you also can set up recurring payments so that bills get paid automatically. The difference is that you, not the vendor, can decide when these recurring payments start and stop.

Of course, this works only for bills that are the same amount every month. Credit cards and other bills that vary require that you specify the amount that gets paid each month.

Online bill paying has another advantage, one shared by automatic charges. Electronic transactions leave excellent "trails" that can show exactly when the bill got paid, so there's never a question of a check getting lost in the mail. If you have a vendor that's constantly slapping you with late fees, and you suspect it's deliberately not processing your check, you can put a stop to those games with electronic payments.

What if none of the solutions thus far works for you? You have one more good option.

Just Pay Your Bills as They Come In

If you sit down and pay each bill immediately as it arrives, most of your worries about late payments will be solved. You'll still need a calendar to keep track of your statements and due dates to make sure a bill hasn't gone awry, but you won't have to worry about losing a notice in a pile of other paperwork.

Step 3: Pay Down Your Debt

Remember that the second most heavily weighted factor in credit scoring is how much of your available credit you're actually using. The lower your balances compared to your credit limits, the better.

The score gauges how much of your limit you use on each card or other revolving line of credit, as well as how much of your combined credit limits you're using on all your cards. The score also factors in any progress you're making on paying down installment accounts such as auto loans and mortgages.

Paying down your debt over time is a way to show consistent, responsible credit-handling behavior and will boost your score.

What does that mean in practice? Read on.

You Need to Reduce What You Owe Rather Than Just Moving Your Balances Around

You can improve your credit scores in the short run by making sure you're using only a portion of the available credit limit on each credit card account. If you have a large balance on one card, and other cards are sitting empty, it makes sense to transfer some of your debt to the unused card. That's because it's better to have small balances on a few cards than one big balance on a single card. But ultimately, you need to pay down your debt. If you continue to charge on your cards instead of paying down your balances, you're using more and more of your available credit limit—and doing more and more damage to your score.

The way to improve your score is to stop the merry-go-round and start actually making a dent in your debt. To do that, continue reading.

You Might Need to Change Your Approach to Paying Off Debt

The usual advice to debt-ridden consumers is that they should pay off their highest-rate debts first, and use lump sums to retire any bills they can afford to pay off in full. That makes a lot of financial sense, but unfortunately it isn't the fastest way to improve your credit score. Instead, you should do this:

- **Prioritize your debts by how close the balances are to the accounts' credit limits**—If boosting your score is your goal, look for the card or other revolving account that's closest to its limit. After that's paid down below 50 percent or so, you can switch to the card or other account that's the second closest to its limit. Your goal should be to eventually pay off all this debt, continuing in this round-robin fashion.

- **Consider a personal loan**—Personal loans typically offer fixed rates and equal monthly payments over their term, which is typically three years. Using a personal loan to pay off credit cards can save you money, if the interest rate is lower, and improve your scores lowering your credit utilization on those all-important revolving accounts. Paying down the installment loan over time will help your scores, too. Your best option for one of these loans is likely your local credit union. Beware of fly-by-night and predatory lenders offering "debt consolidation" loans. In fact:

- **Avoid consolidating your debts**—Many people want to transfer their balances to a single card, either to take advantage of a low rate or for the convenience of having only one due date and interest rate to worry about. But for credit scoring purposes, it's typically better to have small balances on a number of cards than a large balance on one card or other revolving line of credit. That's because the score looks at the gap between the balance and the limit on each card, as well as on all your cards put together.

If you think all this doesn't apply to you because you never carry a balance, think again.

You Need to Pay Attention to How Much You Charge—Even if You Pay Off Your Balances in Full Every Month

As noted in Chapter 2, "How Credit Scoring Works," the credit bureaus—and thus your credit scores—don't differentiate between the balances you pay off and those you carry from month to month. The balances that are reported to the bureaus are typically the ones that show up on the monthly statements you're sent; although sometimes creditors will pick a day of the month and report the balance on that day. Either way, even if you pay off your bill in full the day your statement arrives, you will likely still have balances showing on your credit report, and those will be factored into your score.

Now, paying your balances in full every month is an excellent financial habit. If you're not doing it already, that should be your goal. Not carrying a balance can save you hundreds, if not thousands, of dollars a year in interest payments. Besides, carrying a balance leaves you vulnerable to all kinds of nasty creditor tricks, like having your credit limit suddenly slashed, which has become increasingly common as credit card issuers try to limit their risk.

But even if you can and do pay your balances off, you need to pay attention to how much you're charging each month. You need to stay below—well below—your credit limits.

You know by now that you shouldn't max out your cards or come anywhere close to your credit limits. But the amount of your credit limit you should be using might surprise you.

Your balances (the amount you carry plus the amount you charge) shouldn't exceed about 30 percent of your total credit limit at any given time. The higher your score, the lower the percentage of your credit limits you would need to use to improve your numbers. If your score is already in the high 700s or 800s, you might need to use 10 percent or less of your limit to boost your score.

If you regularly use more than that but can pay off your balance in full every month, there's an easy way to make sure your charging habits don't hurt your score: Simply pay your balance off before it's reported to the bureaus.

Start with your credit reports to see if the balances being reported match those from your last statement. If so, use that statement to find the usual "closing date" for your cards. (It's usually around the same time each month, give or take a few days.) The balance that you owe on this closing date is what typically gets reported to the credit bureaus. If you go online a few days prior to this closing date and pay off your bill, the balance that's reported to the bureaus will be dramatically reduced.

If the balance reported to the credit bureaus isn't the same as your latest statement balance, just call the issuer to ask when your balance gets reported. Then pay a few days before.

Just make sure that you pay any balance still owing when you get your bill. Otherwise, you'll owe finance charges, and your company might even report you as late because they didn't receive a payment after the closing date.

Finally, beware of cards that don't report your credit limit. (Capital One, a leading card issuer, used to be notorious for this; it finally changed its practice after considerable consumer outcry.) When no credit limit is reported to a credit bureau, the scoring formulas typically use the highest balance charged as a proxy. If you regularly charge about the same amount, it can look like you're maxing out your card even if you use only a fraction of your available credit. For example, if your limit is actually $10,000 but you typically charge about $2,000—with the highest amount ever charged about $2,500—the formula could show you using 80 percent of that card's limit ($2,000 divided by $2,500), rather than the 20 percent you're actually using.

You can "solve" this problem by racking up a really big bill one month, thus resetting the highest balance. A better course might be to simply use a card that properly reports your limit.

This isn't a problem for charge cards, like the traditional American Express cards that don't have a preset limit but require you to pay in full every month. The FICO formula ropes off charge card information so that it doesn't affect your credit utilization numbers. But other cards that boast "no preset spending" limit can mess with your scores, so be careful about how you use them.

How to Find Money to Pay Down Your Debt

Paying down debt is a lot like losing weight—easier said than done. But most people can find ways to trim their expenses, boost their incomes, and free up more money to pay off their debts. Here are just a few examples. You can find many more on Web sites devoted to frugality, such as The Dollar Stretcher at www.stretcher.com, or in books such as Amy Dacyczyn's *The Tightwad Gazette.*

- **You can sell stuff**—Hold a yard sale, take clothes to consignment shops, sell unneeded vehicles, and auction off surplus items on eBay. The money generated might go a long way toward paying off your debts.

- **You can trim your spending**—The easiest ways to save are to eat out less often, shop using a grocery list, and entertain yourself at home rather than going out, but you probably can find several other places in your budget to trim. Personal finance software such as Quicken or sites like Mint.com can help you track your spending, but you also can try just writing down every penny you spend for a couple of weeks. You're bound to find little ways that money leaks out of your wallet. Stop those holes, and you can redirect the savings toward debt.

- **You can moonlight**—Few people would want to hold two jobs for long, but you might be able to handle it for several months or however long it takes to put a dent in your debt.

Step 4: Don't Close Credit Cards or Other Revolving Accounts

If your goal is to improve your credit score, don't close any of your current accounts. Closing credit cards and other revolving accounts can *never* help your score, and it might actually hurt it.

Shutting down accounts reduces your total available credit, and that makes your balances loom larger. That narrowing of the gap between the credit you're using and the total credit available to you is one of the things that can hurt your score.

Closing older accounts can also hurt you because the formula notes both the age of your oldest account and the average age of all your accounts. It's particularly important to keep your oldest account active because shutting it could make your credit history look years younger than it actually is—and your score could drop as a result.

It may not be enough, by the way, to keep your oldest credit card in a drawer. If you don't charge something occasionally, your lender could decide the inactive account is more trouble than it's worth and close it for you. To keep it active, you might want to charge some small, recurring bill to the card—a newspaper subscription, your health club dues—and arrange to have the balance paid off automatically each month.

Step 5: Apply for Credit Sparingly

Responsible credit users don't apply for credit they don't need. They also try to pace their credit requests, so that they're not opening a bunch of accounts in a short period of time.

Although your first few credit accounts serve to build and improve your credit history, there typically comes a point when each subsequent credit application can reduce your score. Where that point is, no one knows for sure; all Fair Isaac will say is that it depends on the other information in your file.

That shouldn't keep you from applying for a car loan or getting or refinancing a mortgage. But you should try to resist the urge to apply for a bunch of those "instant" accounts retail stores are always pushing. Sure, you might save 10 percent on your current purchase, but you could wind up paying more in overall interest if too many such applications lower your score.

How to Get a Credit Score if You Don't Have Credit

You might have heard that you need credit to get credit. It can certainly feel that way if you've ever applied for credit and been turned down for lack of a credit history.

But people establish credit all the time, and you can do so fairly quickly if you take the following steps.

If you're a parent with a teen, you might want to help your child through this process as a way to teach her responsible credit use. As noted later, your student will be able to get credit when she is in college; more than 80 percent of college students have at least one card. The best time for students to learn about credit is while they're at home, under your supervision—and long before they pass by their first credit card sign-up booth on campus.

Check Your Credit Report, if You Have One

You might think you have no record at the credit bureaus, but you could be wrong.

Charles, an 18-year-old in Moline, Illinois, was turned down when he applied for his first credit card. He pulled his report and was shocked to find a collection action. It turns out that his parents had placed a newspaper ad for him while he was still a minor and then forgot to pay the bill.

The collection never should have appeared on his report. Minors typically can't be held to contracts and, therefore, are usually not responsible for debts. But the time to detect and fix the problem was before Charles applied for credit.

Another problem you might run into is identity theft. Part of the surge of recent ID fraud cases involves thieves who use children's Social Security numbers to get credit, said Robert Ellis Smith, editor of *Privacy Journal*. This kind of theft can go on for years before being detected.

If that's happened to you, you need to clean up your credit report before trying to apply for new accounts. See Chapter 8 for help.

Set Up Checking and Savings Accounts

These usually don't show up on your credit report, but lenders see them as important signs of financial responsibility and stability. They are also one of the few steps you can take as a minor to start building a financial history because you won't be able to apply for credit in your own name until you are 18.

Getting a debit card can give you some practice in using plastic. Debit cards are ATM cards with a Visa or MasterCard logo. You can use them with a personal identification number, or PIN, or you can use them like a credit card just by signing a charge slip. The amounts you charge are deducted directly from your checking account.

Nan Mead, communications director for the National Endowment for Financial Education, got her son a debit card in the sixth grade. She put a month's worth of money into the account at a time and made him responsible for managing his allowance, lunch money, and incidental expenses, such as haircuts and school supplies:

> *"As I knew he would, he went through the first month's money during his first week of school. He bought CDs, pizza for all of his friends,"*
> *Mead said. "I declined to bail him out, so he ended up taking a sack lunch to school for the rest of the month—a very uncool thing to do at that age, of course—and he had no discretionary money left to spend, either. His money management skills improved each month, though, until, by Christmas, he was doing quite well, even saving for some short-term goals."*

As a college freshman, Mead's son received a credit card with a $500 limit, which worked out well:

> *"In retrospect, the debit card was probably one of the best things I've done, in terms of providing a financial lesson to my son," Mead said.*
> *"The mistakes he made initially were small, in the overall scheme of things, and he learned from them. When he graduates to one or more unrestricted credit cards, I believe he will do just fine."*

Use Someone Else's Good Name

You might be able to jump-start your credit history by being added to some-one else's credit card as an authorized or joint user. Many issuers will import the history for that account onto your credit report. (Before you take this step, have the account holder call the credit card company to make sure such an import will happen. Some issuers import only the account history when the new person is added as a joint user or is a spouse, whereas others don't have that restriction.)

Being added as a joint or authorized user can be a wonderful boost if the person who's adding you is responsible with credit. If not, though, the results can be disastrous.

Angie P., a Kansas college student, learned that the hard way. Her moth-er added her as a joint user on a credit card and then failed to pay the bill for more than two months when money grew tight over the holidays. Angie only discovered the delinquency when she checked her credit report:

"I'm just worried an employer will look at my [credit reports] and think I'm irresponsible because of this mess!" Angie said. "What's worse— I'm an accounting and finance major, and this makes it look like I don't know how to handle my money."

If you're added as an authorized user, you're not responsible for paying the bill. But the original user's mistakes could still show up in your credit file. So if your goal is to establish good credit quickly, pick someone who has been responsible with credit and is likely to continue that behavior in the future.

Another strategy to start a credit history is to get someone with good credit to cosign a loan with you. The cosigner is taking a considerable risk because if you fail to pay, the delinquencies show up on the other person's credit report. But sometimes soft-hearted relatives or friends are willing to take this chance.

Consider Applying for Credit While You're a College Student

Before the Credit Card Accountability Responsibility and Disclosure Act of 2009, getting a credit card as a college student was a breeze. In fact, it was a lot easier to get an unsecured card in school than it was after you graduated. Lenders knew your parents were likely to pay your bills if you couldn't—and that parental support typically ends with graduation.

One reader told me that she lectured her daughter against the evils of credit cards and advised her to steer clear while she was in college. After the younger woman got out of school, though, the very lenders who had been falling all over themselves to offer her cards were now turning down her applications.

After certain provisions of the CARD Act took effect in 2010, though, the picture changed. The law now says people under 21 can't get a card unless a parent, guardian, or spouse is willing to cosign, or the young adult shows proof of sufficient income to cover the credit obligation. Offering students "tangible gifts" like Frisbees and T-shirts was banned, as was marketing cards on campus.

Borrowers and issuers have found some ways around the law. Some students report their student loan checks as "income," while some banks have switched from Frisbees to coupons or $50 statement credits as inducements to sign up.

If you do apply for a card, choose it carefully. Look for the lowest available annual fee and interest rate. And don't go overboard—one or two major bankcards (Visa, MasterCard, American Express, or Discover) should be enough for now.

Apply for an Alternative Card

If you can't get a regular credit card, consider applying for a gas or department store charge card, which are typically fairly easy to get.

You also might consider a secured credit card. These cards require that you make a deposit with a bank (usually $200 to $1,000), and your credit limit is typically limited to that deposit amount. The best cards don't charge application fees, have low annual fees, and convert to a regular, unsecured card after a year or so. Web sites, such as Bankrate.com, CreditCards.com, and CardRatings.com, among others, offer lists of secured cards, including their rates and terms.

Make sure in advance that the lender reports to the credit bureaus. You can't build a credit history if the lender isn't reporting your payments.

Get an Installment Loan

After you've used plastic responsibly for several months, you might try for a small auto or personal loan. Because the credit-scoring formula wants to see that you can responsibly handle different types of credit, adding an installment loan to your mix of credit cards can boost your score.

Amanda got her first credit card at 18, two weeks after she moved out of her parents' house. The card had a $200 limit and an atrocious 19.8 percent interest rate, but Amanda used it strictly to build her credit history by buying groceries and paying the bill off in full each month.

After six months, she got a credit card with a more reasonable interest rate and a higher limit. Three months after that, she got a used car loan for $6,000:

> *"Not bad for an 18-year-old," she said. "A year later, I got a gold credit card with a 12.9 percent [interest rate]."*

Today, Amanda checks her credit reports and scores every three months. She enjoys watching her credit score rise, and it motivates her to continue her good financial habits. She just wished more of her peers knew what she knows:

> *"If parents would address the credit issues with their children," Amanda said, "and explain the importance of establishing a good credit history and of using credit wisely and responsibly, then maybe there wouldn't be so many problems."*

Credit Scores Without Credit

Lenders know there's a big market of the "credit underserved"—people with nonexistent or thin credit histories. Fair Isaac estimates that more than 50 million Americans either have no credit bureau files or have too little information in their files to generate a FICO credit score.

Those hoping to tap this market have experimented with alternative approaches to gauging creditworthiness, such as monitoring whether an applicant has paid rent or utilities on time. In mid-2004, Fair Isaac introduced the FICO Expansion Score, which uses nontraditional information sources to create credit scores for people who don't already have credit. These sources include bounced-check monitoring companies and retail purchase payment plans, such as rent-to-own programs. Fair Isaac says it has enough of this nontraditional data to provide scores of half of the underserved population, or 25 million people. Other companies have invented similar systems that try to gauge the creditworthiness of folks who don't yet have credit.

Experian made a big splash in December 2010 when it announced it was adding rent payment data to its credit bureaus but failed to add the caveat that such information wouldn't be picked up by FICO credit scoring formulas.

Still, the expansion of credit and credit scoring into new realms is likely to continue. And that just underlines how important it is to adopt responsible money habits, such as paying your bills on time and managing your bank accounts. You never know who might be watching.

5

Credit-Scoring Myths

For most of credit scoring's history, the vast majority of the people involved in lending decisions pretty much had to guess what hurt or helped a score. Creators of scoring formulas didn't want to reveal much about how the models worked, for fear that competitors would steal their ideas or that consumers would figure out how to beat the system.

Fortunately, today we know a lot more about credit scoring—but not everybody has kept up with the latest intelligence. Some of the worst misinformation comes from self-styled experts who purport to know the inside scoop, but who actually promote outdated or downright false ideas about how credit scoring works. Acting on their bad advice can put your score and your finances at significant risk.

Here are some of the most common myths.

Myth 1: Closing Credit Accounts Will Help Your Score

This one sounds logical, especially when a mortgage broker tells you that lenders are suspicious of people who have a lot of unused credit available to them. What's to keep you, after all, from rushing out and charging up a storm?

Of course, if you think about it, what's kept you from racking up big balances before now? If you've been pretty responsible with credit in the past, you're likely to continue to be pretty responsible in the future. That's the basic principle behind credit scoring: It rewards behaviors that show moderate, responsible use of credit over time because those habits are likely to continue.

But many still believe the myth that they'll be punished for having "too many open accounts." And then they compound the error by assuming they can "fix" this problem by closing accounts.

After you've opened the accounts, you've done the damage. You can't undo it by closing the account.

You can, however, make matters worse. Closing accounts can hurt you in two ways:

- Closing accounts reduces the total credit available to you, which can make your credit utilization ratio rise. Remember that the FICO formula measures the gap between the credit you use and your total credit limits. The wider the gap, the better. If you suddenly lower that limit by shutting down accounts, the gap narrows—and that can be a bad thing. This is true whether you keep a balance on your credit cards or you pay them off in full every month. Remember: The FICO formula doesn't differentiate between balances that are carried and those that are paid off.

- Closing accounts can eventually make your credit history look younger than it is. Your credit score factors in the age of your oldest account and the average age of all your accounts. So closing accounts, particularly older accounts, can ding your score eventually; although the effect is typically much less dramatic than that inflicted by a changing credit utilization ratio.

In reality, closing revolving credit accounts can almost *never* help your score, and it might well hurt it.

In the past, I would get flooded with emails every time I wrote about this fact, insisting I was wrong. But every time Fair Isaac has investigated a case where a lending professional claimed a closure helped a score, it discovered that some other factor was actually responsible.

Sometimes the change was fairly obvious, such as a negative mark that passed the seven-year limitation and was dropped from the report. More often, the difference in scores was the result of something subtler, such as lower balances being reported on the borrower's accounts or the simple passage of time. (Remember: The longer it's been since you opened your first account and your last account, and the longer you've been paying on time, the better the effect on your score.)

This doesn't mean that you should never close a credit card or other revolving account. You might want to get rid of a card that's charging you an annual fee or shut down a few unused accounts to reduce the chances they could be hijacked by an identity thief. If your FICO score is already in the mid-700s or higher, you should be fine closing a few accounts; although you might want to keep your oldest or highest-limit cards. Otherwise, though, you'd be smart just to leave accounts open until your score improves.

There are other good reasons to close accounts. If you have a serious spending problem, you might find cutting up and canceling your credit cards is the only way to keep yourself in line. If that's true, your credit score is probably the least of your worries.

You also might encounter one of those lenders who is spooked by open credit card accounts and demands that you close some. If the loan is big enough, like a mortgage, and the lender has already committed to giving you the money, you might have to take the risk to get your loan. But don't close accounts as a preemptive measure and endanger your score.

Myth 2: You Can Boost Your Score by Asking Your Credit Card Company to Lower Your Limits

This one is a variation on the idea that reducing your available credit somehow helps your score by making you seem less risky to lenders. Once again, it's off the mark.

Narrowing the gap between the credit you use and the credit you have available to you can have a negative effect on your score. It doesn't matter that you asked for the reduction; the FICO formula doesn't distinguish between lower limits that you requested and lower limits imposed by a creditor. All it sees is less space between your balances and your limits, and that's not good.

If you want to help your score, tackle the problem from the other end: by paying down your debt. Increasing the gap between your balance and your credit limit has a positive effect on your score.

Myth 3: You Can Hurt Your Score by Checking Your Own Credit Report

Hans, a doctor, emailed me in a panic after talking with his lender:

"I heard from our mortgage officer at our state employees' credit union that if you access your credit report too often—even just to clean it up—it looks unfavorable to lenders. How can I then run a check safely to clean it up in preparation for our 'dream home' mortgage?"

Shortly after receiving that email, I received this perky little admonition from Lisa in East Wenatchee, Washington—yet another misinformed "expert":

"As a real estate agent with 20+ years of sales experience, I appreciate the information you shared [on CNBC today] with the home-buying consumer. However, your advice for the consumer to check their 'credit report often...' needs to be modified. Each and every time consumers check their credit reports, it actually lowers their credit scores! I have had clients check their credit on a weekly basis, only to have their FICO scores lowered by as much as 50 points!!!"

No amount of exclamation points makes it so, Lisa. Next to the myth about closing accounts, the myth that you can hurt your score just by checking your credit report seems to be the most pervasive—and potentially destructive.

You need to check your credit report and your score fairly frequently to make sure all is right with your financial world. Checking once a year is about the minimum; given the prevalence of identity theft, you might want to check in with all three bureaus at least twice a year. You should definitely pull all three reports and scores a few months before applying for new credit, because it can take awhile to correct any errors you find.

The folks at Fair Isaac understand your need to review your own data, which is why the FICO formula ignores any inquiries generated when you check your own reports and scores. The same is true of VantageScores.

Where you can hurt yourself is if you ask a lender to check your score. When a lender pulls your credit, it generates what's known as a "hard" inquiry—and that is counted against your score.

As long as you order from a credit bureau or a service affiliated with a bureau, such as MyFico.com, your inquiries won't hurt your score.

Myth 4: You Can Hurt Your Score by Shopping Around for the Best Rates

The folks propagating this particular myth might have an ulterior motive. After all, if you don't know what the competition is offering, how will you know whether you got a good deal?

Creators of scoring formulas know that smart consumers want to shop around for the best rates, particularly on cars and homes. That's why the FICO formulas ignore all mortgage- and auto-related inquiries made within a certain period. If the formula finds any inquiries before that period, it lumps together any auto- or mortgage-related ones made within a certain period. (Older versions of the FICO formula use a 14-day period, whereas newer versions use 30 or 45 days.) In effect, if you had six mortgage inquiries and three auto inquiries within that short time frame, the formula would count only two inquiries total. So if you do your shopping for a car loan or mortgage in a concentrated period of time and get the loan before the window is up, you should be fine. Even if it takes a little longer to get your loan approved, as often happens with mortgages, you should be okay if your rate shopping was confined to a relatively short period.

What you don't want to do is drag out the process over several weeks or apply for credit cards right before you plan to get a mortgage or a car loan. The "deduplification" process—that's what Fair Isaac calls it—only gives special treatment to inquiries that are car- or mortgage-related. You'd also be wise not to shop for car loans while you're looking for a mortgage, or vice versa, because the formula lumps mortgage and auto inquiries separately.

You can protect yourself further and make the shopping process easier by doing some research before you contact any lenders. Get your reports and scores so that you know where you stand, and then check Internet sites, such as MyFico.com or Bankrate.com, to see the kind of rates you can expect to get, given your score. That way you'll be able to tell a good deal from a bad one when it's offered.

By the way, speaking of bad deals, you should be careful not to give any credit or other personal financial information to a car dealership until you're ready to buy the car. Readers have reported finding dozens of inquiries on their credit reports after having casually visited a dealership or two. Although multiple inquiries made on the same day might not affect your score that much because they're all lumped together by the FICO formula, a page of inquiries might unnerve any lender who actually looks at your report.

People who have poor credit need to be particularly vigilant about inquiries. Although someone who has a good score might lose 5 points or so from a single inquiry, the impact can be greater for someone who has a troubled, sparse, or brief credit history. Repeatedly trying for loans and being turned down can take a toll on your score over time. Just read what happened to Chris in Asheville, North Carolina:

"Over the years, as I have struggled with my credit, I have tried several times to buy a car. Each time I have applied for credit, the car lot has run my credit at about 15 different [lenders] trying to get me a loan. Multiply this over the last two years (I know that's how long inquiries stay on your report) times two cars per year, and I have about a page and a half of inquiries. Now, this has had a dramatic effect on my credit score."

Actually, it's highly unlikely that inquiries alone are devastating Chris' score. It's more likely that his past credit troubles are still having an effect. But Chris certainly isn't making things better. Rather than give his score a chance to recover and improve, he keeps trying every six months, inflicting fresh injury.

Because his score is already poor, each new inquiry or group of inquiries is likely to hurt more than it might had he enjoyed a better score.

A better course for Chris and others who have poor scores is to give up on the idea of a car loan for a while and concentrate on improving their FICOs. Paying their bills on time, paying down any debt they have, and getting and using a secured credit card should help their scores. After their numbers are out of the cellar, they can shop for loans without drastically impacting their scores.

Myth 5: You Don't Have to Use Credit to Get a Good Credit Score

Some people are so suspicious of credit that they advise giving up credit cards and living on a cash-only basis. They acknowledge that most people need mortgages and auto loans, but they feel the best way to impress a lender is by living a credit-free life.

Now that you know something about how credit scoring works, you can see the holes in this theory. The credit-scoring formula is designed to judge how well you handle credit over time. If you have no credit, or you don't at least occasionally use the credit you have, the formula won't have enough information to make an assessment. You don't have to live in *debt* to get a decent score, but you do need to use credit.

In the past, some people were able to get high credit scores without having much credit. Earlier incarnations of the FICO credit score gave scores over 700 to some people with just one or two recently opened accounts. The newer versions of the formula, however, make it much tougher to get a lofty score if you have a thin credit history.

So-called "alternate" scores also confuse some people about what helps to get credit. FICO and other score creators have been working on formulas that use non-traditional data, such as utility bills and address changes, to attempt to score more people. They're trying to help lenders reach the "underserved" market that may not have credit accounts but could be good credit risks. These scores are not in widespread use, though, so the traditional ways of building credit by using credit are still the best.

You probably need to be concerned about your score even if you have no plans to take out loans. Now that insurers are using credit information for underwriting and rating decisions, your failure to maintain a credit history could cost you in the form of higher premiums.

It's too bad that conscientious people who simply don't like debt should be punished with higher premiums, and some states have even banned insurers from using a lack of credit history as a reason to raise rates. If your state hasn't prohibited the practice, though, you might want to dust off your credit card and use it once in awhile.

Myth 6: You Have to Pay Interest to Have a Good Credit Score

This is the exact opposite of the preceding myth, and it's just as misguided.

You don't need to carry a balance on your credit cards and pay interest to have a good score. As you've read several times already, your credit reports—and thus the FICO formula—make no distinction between balances you carry month to month and balances you pay off. Smart consumers don't carry credit card balances for any reason, and certainly not to improve their scores.

Now, it is true that to get the highest FICO scores, you need to have both *revolving accounts*, such as credit cards, and *installment loans*, such as a mortgage or car loan. And with the exception of those 0 percent rates used to push auto sales, most installment loans require paying interest.

But here's a news flash: You don't need to have the *very highest score* to get good credit. Any score over 720 or so is going to get you the best rates and terms with many lenders. Some, particularly auto and home equity lenders, reserve their best deals for those with scores over 760. You don't have to have an 850, or even 800 score, to get great deals.

If you're trying to improve a mediocre score, a small, affordable installment loan can help—provided that you can get approved for it and pay it off on time. But otherwise there's no reason to get yourself into debt and pay interest.

Myth 7: Adding a 100-Word Statement to Your File Can Help Your Score if You Have an Unresolved Dispute with a Lender

Dave in Los Angeles wound up in a protracted fight with his phone company, which for months billed him for a phone line that, in fact, never worked. He went round and round with the company's technical service, customer service, and billing department. Finally, he gave up, refusing to pay the bill—even when it went into collections and onto his credit report. Dave figured he could offset the damage to his credit by sending the credit bureaus a 100-word statement explaining the problem.

Federal law does give you the right to have such statements attached to your credit file. Unfortunately, the credit-scoring formula can't read—at least not in the traditional sense. It calculates scores based on how items on your credit report are coded, and these 100-word statements aren't coded at all, so they're not counted.

It's not clear how helpful such statements were before credit scoring became so widespread, but they're certainly not much help now.

Given how damaging late payments, collections, and other recent negative marks are on your score, you want to avoid them if at all possible. This doesn't necessarily mean you have to give in and pay a bill that's clearly in error. But you also shouldn't let a $30 spat with your book club escalate into a collection that could trash your score. You might have to pay the bill under protest and then sue the vendor in small claims court.

Fortunately, most credit disputes can be solved well short of that. If you used a credit card to purchase something that didn't work, you can use the credit card company's dispute-resolution process as outlined on the back of your statements. Patient, polite persistence with a company's customer service department can also help, as can a willingness to seek out supervisors or regulators who might be able to cut through a log jam.

If the collection has already landed on your report, follow the steps in Chapter 7, "Rebuilding Your Score After a Credit Disaster," to minimize or eliminate the impact.

Myth 8: Your Closed Accounts Should Read "Closed by Consumer," or They Will Hurt Your Score

The theory behind this myth is that lenders will see a closed account on your credit report and, if not informed otherwise, will assume that a disgusted creditor cut you off because you screwed up somehow.

Of course, as you know by now, many lenders never see your actual report. They're just looking at your credit score, which couldn't care less who closed a credit card. Fair Isaac figures that if a lender shuts down your account, it's either for inactivity or because you defaulted. If you defaulted, that will be amply documented in the account's history.

If it makes you feel better to contact the bureaus and ensure that accounts you closed are listed as "closed by consumer," by all means do so. But it won't make any difference to your credit score.

Myth 9: Credit Counseling Is Worse Than Bankruptcy

Sometimes this is phrased as "credit counseling is as bad as bankruptcy" or "credit counseling is as bad as Chapter 13 bankruptcy." None of these statements is true.

A bankruptcy filing is the single worst thing you can do to your credit score. By contrast, the FICO formula completely ignores any reference to credit counseling that might be on your credit report. Credit counseling is treated as a neutral factor, neither helping nor harming your score.

Credit counselors, in case you're not familiar with the term, specialize in working out payment plans for debtors who might otherwise file for bankruptcy. Although credit counselors might consolidate the consumer's bills into one monthly payment, they don't offer loans—as debt consolidators do—or promise to eliminate or settle debts for less than the principal amount you owe.

The fact that credit counseling itself won't affect your score does not mean, however, that enrolling in a credit counselor's debt management plan will leave your credit unscathed.

Some lenders will report you as late just for enrolling in a debt management plan. Their reasoning is that you're not paying them what you originally owed, so you should have to suffer some pain.

That's not the only way you could be reported late. As you'll read in the next chapter, not all credit counselors are created equal, and some have been accused of withholding consumer payments that were intended for creditors. The missing payments showed up as "lates" on the consumers' credit reports, hurting their scores.

Finally, some lenders—particularly mortgage lenders—do indeed view current participation in a credit counseling program as the equivalent of a Chapter 13 bankruptcy. If they see it mentioned on a credit report, they won't extend credit as long as the notation of credit counseling remains on the borrower's file. But typically such notations are dropped as soon as the borrower completes the repayment plan. By contrast, a Chapter 13 bankruptcy can be reported for seven years or more. (A Chapter 7 bankruptcy, which involves erasing your debts rather than retiring them with a repayment plan, stays on your report for up to ten years.)

Credit counseling isn't something you should sign up for just because you want a lower interest rate or one place to send your payments instead of many. But, if you're behind on your debts or can pay only the minimums, and you want an alternative to bankruptcy, you shouldn't stay away because of myths about its long-term impact on your credit.

Myth 10: Bankruptcy Hurts Your Score So Much That It's Impossible to Get Credit

Bankruptcy does deal a devastating blow to your score, but that doesn't mean you can't get credit afterward.

How quickly you'll reestablish credit and how much you'll pay for it will depend largely on your behavior after you file for bankruptcy, as well as how lenders overall are feeling about risk. If you start handling credit responsibly—paying your bills on time, not running up big balances, and not applying for a bunch of credit at once—your score will begin to recover.

But it also will matter which lenders you approach for credit. Many mainstream lenders shun people who have filed for bankruptcy—sometimes just for the first few years, although sometimes for as long as the bankruptcy remains on your file.

Lenders also can change their policies, becoming more tolerant of credit glitches when they want to attract more customers and less tolerant when their losses climb. During and after the 2008 financial crisis, defaults spiked so much that many lenders dramatically raised their credit standards, which made it harder to recover from setbacks.

In good economic times, it can be fairly easy for people who filed bankruptcy to get new credit.

John, a military man stationed in Texas, said he and his wife were able to buy a house one year after their Chapter 7 bankruptcy filing and were approved for other accounts, including a credit card and a cell phone. Buying a car has proved more of a challenge:

> *"It doesn't seem like my credit score is increasing at all. I say that*
> *because I applied to buy a Jeep last week and got turned down.*
> *A couple of months ago, I tried to buy a motorcycle and was*
> *turned down. What else can I do to increase my score?"*

Actually, the couple's credit scores probably were increasing—they just hadn't gotten high enough for a mainstream auto lender to take a chance. Chris of Knoxville tried a different approach after filing for bankruptcy along with his wife:

> *"About two months after our discharge, we tried to buy a used car.*
> *We tried about five different banks and were turned down by each one,"*
> *Chris wrote. "A couple of months later, Saturn was having a*
> *'second-chance' type of sale [for people with troubled credit].*
> *We were able to purchase at a higher interest rate. We were*
> *a little disappointed [at the rate] but grateful that we were*
> *able to purchase a nice family car to rebuild our credit."*

Corey of Hermitage, Tennessee, filed for bankruptcy in 2001. Within two years, Corey had graduated from secured credit cards (which require a deposit) to regular credit cards and auto loans:

> *"Sure, it has been very hard to get credit sometimes. The only credit card*
> *I could get [at first] was one from Providian Financial, and even then*
> *it had to be a secured one; however, the pain has been worth it. I have*

since turned that secured credit card into an unsecured one. Providian issued me another [card], and then Merrick Bank issued me one. I have also been able to acquire two car loans, my most recent one for my 2001 Nissan Xterra for $23,000 and at a 10 percent interest rate.

The rates on my car loan and credit card could be better; however, I have no financial debt now other than my car and student loans, and I even have a great-paying job with some money in the bank now."

These days, people with a bankruptcy on their record may need more patience. Far fewer lenders cater to those with troubled credit, so rebuilding credit can take more time. For more information about how best to rebuild after bankruptcy or other credit disaster, see Chapter 6, "Coping with a Credit Crisis."

Can You Get a Mortgage Without Credit Scores

Broadcast personality Dave Ramsey calls credit scores "debt lovers' scores" and has assured his audiences that they're not necessary to get a mortgage. But the home lender he endorses, Churchill Mortgages, tells a rather different story.

Right off the bat, Churchill Mortgage warns people on its Web site that getting a mortgage approved without credit scores is "downright tough."

"That may not be what you wanted to hear, but it is what you need to know before getting your hopes way up," the site explains.

Would-be borrowers have the best chance if they have a 20 percent down payment, can afford a 15-year repayment term, and have at least four alternative tradelines such as rent payments, cell phone bills, insurance payments, and utilities, the site explains.

Underwriting a nontraditional mortgage takes about three times as long as processing a "normal borrower file," Churchill explains, which is why most lenders won't bother. Even when such a lender is found, borrowers without credit scores aren't guaranteed a loan—far from it:

"The few lenders that will still do these loans can decide to stop taking these loans at any time—even when the loan is in underwriting—and leave the borrower with no other option. Sound scary and unpredictable? It can be. That is why we want to fully inform you of the risks involved so those that have no credit score and start the loan process can know in advance how unpredictable this loan process can be."

That scary, unpredictable process is a sharp contrast to what people with good credit scores face, which is a market teeming with eager lenders offering competitive rates.

If you still want to try for a mortgage without having credit scores, Churchill recommends including "strong protective contingencies" in a home purchase contract so that you can get your earnest money back if your loan isn't approved. The stronger the protective contingencies, though, the less attractive your offer may be—especially in hot markets where many buyers can get their loans approved quickly.

So the answer to the question "Can you get a mortgage without credit scores?" is "Maybe—but if you have a choice, why would you want to?"

6

Coping with a Credit Crisis

A credit crisis—being unable to manage your debts—can come on slowly as the result of overspending for many years. The balances on your accounts grow and grow; pretty soon you're able to make only the minimum payments, and then not even that.

Other times a credit crisis comes at you in a rush as a result of another financial setback—a job loss, a divorce, a major illness. Suddenly, you have more "outgo" than "income," and you're not sure where to turn.

Or your crisis could be the result of larger financial turmoil. After years of encouraging people to borrow money, lenders began sharply cutting back their risk in 2008 as a result of the financial crisis. They raised rates, chopped lines of credit, and closed or froze accounts. People who once enjoyed cheap credit, and plenty of it, suddenly found themselves with much higher rates and nowhere to turn. The situation worsened as the financial crisis rippled through the economy, throwing millions of people out of work and causing home values to plummet.

Many people facing credit and financial problems are hoping for some quick, magical fix. Some ask whether they should get a debt consolidation loan, use credit counseling, or tap their retirement funds. Jeff of Fair Lawn, New Jersey, is fairly typical. At 44, he's accumulated more than $40,000 in credit card debt and is finding it tough to pay much more than the minimum balances he owes:

> *"I am seriously considering a disbursement [from a prior employer's 401(k)] to pay off my credit card bills. I understand there would be 20 percent withheld immediately, and a 10 percent early withdraw penalty next year at tax time. I'm still young enough to put future earnings aside for my retirement. I'm ready to make the leap. Am I wrong with this assessment? So much cash goes from my income straight to the credit card banks that it seems to be a viable alternative. What do you think?"*

Kathy of Chapel Hill, North Carolina, had $20,000 in credit card debt, racked up during a tumultuous period when her husband became disabled, a parent died, and she lost her job. She had enough equity in her home to pay the debt, but she can't find a lender willing to lend her the money to refinance:

> *"I have a horrible credit report," she emailed. "I missed two months of credit card payments when Dad died, and the balances are high. [I could] sell the house... but, boy, I hate to move. This farmhouse is our only stability, as is our neighborhood."*

The truth is that there frequently are no easy fixes when you're in a credit crisis. Even solutions that seem like a silver bullet often end up having unintended consequences: on your pocketbook, to your credit score, and as to your future financial options.

How you handle credit problems will have a huge effect not only on your credit worthiness, but also on your financial future. The wrong move can sink you further into debt, devastate what's left of your scores, and put your entire financial life at risk. The right moves can help you climb out of the hole stronger, wealthier, and more creditworthy than ever before.

If you're in the midst of a crisis, you need to get to work right away to minimize the damage, evaluate your options, and steer your financial ship away from the rocks.

If you've already endured the crisis and are getting back on your feet, you can skip ahead to the next chapter—but you might find some important information here that could help prevent a future catastrophe.

The steps you need to take are fairly straightforward:

1. **Figure out how to free up some cash**—You might not
    need to tap every source of income you identify, but it's
    good to know what's available before you go any further.

2. **Evaluate your options**—If you find enough cash, you
    might be able to set up a repayment plan and put the crisis
    behind you. If you don't, you have an array of tough but
    important choices to consider.

3. **Choose a path and take action**—You might not like all
    the consequences you'll have to face, but further delay
    will simply make matters worse. The quicker you pick
    a plan and get started, the sooner your credit can start to
    recover.

Before you get started, you'll want some breathing room—psychological
"space," if you will—to deal with your financial problems. If you're stressed
over bills, give yourself permission to take a deep breath, and know that by
the end of this process, you'll have a plan. If you and your partner have been
fighting over money, try to declare a truce while you get things sorted out.

If debt collectors are hounding you, you have the legal right to send them
a letter telling them not to contact you, and they're required to comply.

Unfortunately, some collection agencies have taken to filing lawsuits
against consumers who send them such letters or who refuse to answer their
calls. They figure if you won't talk to them on the phone, they'll get your
attention by dragging you to court and suing you over your debts. That, of
course, can make your current problems even worse.

If debt collectors are making your life miserable or threatening lawsuits,
you should download the free eBook *Debt Collection Answers: How to Use
Debt Collection Laws to Protect Your Rights* by Gerri Detweiler and Mary
Reed, available from DebtCollectionAnswers. com. I provide a few suggestions on dealing with collectors in the next two chapters, but this is a complicated area of finance with laws that vary widely across the country. You
might need additional help that is beyond the scope of this book.

Step 1: Figure Out How to Free Up Some Cash

One of the most common mistakes people make in a financial crisis is not cutting back hard enough, fast enough.

Charlie, an animator, is a classic example. He knew when his last project ended that hundreds of his fellow animators were out of work and that the next job could be a long time coming. But he hoped for the best. He and his wife even continued paying for their children's private schools; in fact, more than a third of the $150,000 they borrowed against their home equity line of credit went for tuition.

"My wife didn't want to disrupt their lives or their schooling," Charlie explained.

This refusal to cut back is far from unique, according to debt expert Steve Rhode, who blogs at GetOutofDebt.org. People in a financial crisis often put off trimming their budgets, hoping something will come along to save them. That kind of optimistic attitude is perfectly human—and can be perfectly disastrous. It doesn't make much sense to insist that you can't possibly take your kids out of private school only to wind up losing your home.

You might not be paying $50,000 for tuition, but chances are you could find plenty of ways to cut your expenses if you got serious. Perhaps you're clinging to a car you can't afford, an expensive cell phone plan, or a habit of eating out.

If you need help finding ways to cut costs, check out some of the many frugality-oriented Web sites, such as The Dollar Stretcher at www.stretcher.com, Get Rich Slowly at www.getrichslowly.org, or The Simple Dollar at www.thesimpledollar.com. You'll also find whole shelves of books on this topic at your local library, with Amy Dacyczyn's *The Complete Tightwad Gazette* the likely centerpiece.

Or maybe you need to take a hard look at some of your bigger bills. Even your so-called fixed expenses, such as your mortgage or rent, aren't really set in stone. Rhode says he often counsels people who struggle to hang on to homes that are simply too expensive for them, when the smarter course would be to move.

Don't panic quite yet. For the moment, you don't have to do anything other than write down the potential savings you can identify. You might find it helpful to break those savings down into three categories:

- **The easy stuff**—Expenses you could ditch with little effort

- **The harder stuff**—Expenses that would require more sacrifice to trim

- **The last-ditch stuff**—Expenses you would cut only as a last resort

Again, at this point we're trying to find potential sources of cash so that you can better evaluate your options. Just don't close your mind to what might seem right now like drastic measures.

There are two other good ways to raise cash: selling stuff and making more money. If you can sell an extra vehicle, hold a yard sale, or auction unused items on eBay, you might free up a good chunk of change. You also might consider freelance work or a second job temporarily. If you're already working full time, this can seem pretty daunting, but you might do something for a few months that you'd never sustain permanently.

You might notice that I haven't included some of the most-touted "fixes" for credit problems: home equity loans, other debt-consolidation loans, and withdrawals or loans from retirement plans. That's because these "solutions," as typically applied, often make matters worse in the long run.

Home equity loans, lines of credit, and cash-out mortgage refinances are particularly seductive because they tend to offer relatively low rates and tax-deductible interest, to boot. But they come with big problems:

- Most people who use home equity to pay off credit card and other unsecured loans ultimately end up deeper in debt within a few years. That's because they haven't changed the fundamental problem of overspending that got them in trouble in the first place.

- Such loans usually turn what should be short-term debt into long-term debt. You could end up paying more in interest—and again, wind up poorer—than if you'd buckled down and just paid off the cards out of your current income.

- Using these loans to pay off credit cards, medical bills, or personal loans turns unsecured debt, which could have been erased in bankruptcy court, into secured debt that can't be wiped out—and that puts your home at risk as well.

Many people who tapped their equity during the boom years found themselves "upside down"—owing more on their homes than they're worth—as house prices plunged.

Most retirement plans are also protected from creditors' claims in bankruptcy court and typically shouldn't be used to pay off unsecured debt. In addition, a withdrawal from a 401(k) or IRA means you're losing out on the tax-deferred returns that your money could earn in the plan if you left it alone. Every $10,000 you take out of a 401(k), for example, could cost you $100,000 or more in future retirement income, assuming it had been left alone to grow at an 8 percent average annual rate for 30 years.

The idea that you would protect your retirement or home equity instead of paying debts outrages some people. They feel every possible source of funds should be tapped to pay off debts you owe. If that's the way you feel, fine. But you should remember that the credit card companies are going to thrive whether or not you pay your bills. How will you thrive in retirement if you've decimated your funds before you even get there? Hopefully, your finances will turn out to be healthy enough that you can pay off all your debts, but you should think twice, and then again, before raiding either your retirement or your home.

In addition to the long-term cost, withdrawals from 401(k)s, IRAs, and other plans typically incur heavy penalties and fees. Come April 15, you would face a tax bill equal to 25 percent to 50 percent of what you took out.

Loans from 401(k)s and 403(b)s have their own dangers: If you lose your job, you typically must repay the loan within a few weeks, or you'll owe penalties and taxes on the balance.

Are there exceptions? Of course. You might decide to borrow from your 401(k) to pay the mortgage for a month or two to avoid foreclosure, for example. But if you can't make your house payment any other way than by tapping your retirement funds, you can't afford your home. You need to consider other alternatives—a regular sale if you have equity, a short sale if you don't, turning the keys over to the bank in a "deed in lieu of foreclosure" exchange, or even letting it go through the foreclosure process. We'll discuss those options more in a bit. In any case, your long-term financial health depends on your fixing these fundamental troubles, not merely delaying the day of reckoning.

As far as debt consolidation loans go, you're almost certainly better off steering clear. There's a lot of consumer abuse, if not outright fraud, in this area. High, hidden fees are common, as are loans that just stretch out your obligation and ultimately cost you more than if you'd paid off the original debt.

A similar warning goes for debt-settlement firms. Many of these outfits promise to settle your debts for pennies on the dollar—often, supposedly, without hurting your credit. In reality, debt-settlement tactics often leave your credit score in shreds, and sometimes the company simply disappears with your big up-front fee. If you choose this option, do plenty of research first.

Steer clear of any outfit that touts "debt-elimination." These scams use cockamamie theories about the Declaration of Independence or "natural law" to argue that you don't really owe what you owe. It's not true, and you could lose thousands in "fees" for this bad advice.

If you really can't pay all of your unsecured debts and your income is below the median for your area, your best bet often is to file for Chapter 7 bankruptcy rather than messing with half measures. You can get a fresh start, and you'll have the money you otherwise would have thrown at these nonstarter "solutions."

If you have unpayable debts and your income is above the median, you may have to choose between a Chapter 13 bankruptcy repayment plan and negotiating settlements with your creditors. If that's the case, get advice from an experienced bankruptcy attorney before you proceed.

Either way, you need to know more about your choices.

Step 2: Evaluating Your Options

This step actually includes a number of other tasks, all of which take a little time but are essential to making sure you choose the right option.

Task 1: Prioritize Your Bills

If you're being hounded by creditors or are simply stressed by debt, it can be easy for your priorities to get out of whack. You might wind up paying a credit card bill when the rent or mortgage is due just because a collection agency is making your life miserable. You'd be risking eviction or foreclosure over a bill that could be wiped out in bankruptcy court, or at least postponed without major consequences.

You need to be the one deciding how your bills get paid without undue outside pressure.

Once again, we'll be dividing into threes: essential bills, important bills, and nonessential bills.

Essential bills are the ones that, if you don't pay, will result in catastrophic consequences.

The Bill	The Consequence for Not Paying
Mortgage or rent	Foreclosure or eviction
Home equity loans or lines of credit	Foreclosure or eviction
Groceries	Starvation
Utilities	Absence of lights, heat, water, or phone
Child care	Child evicted from care; possible lost job
Payments on a car needed for work	Lost job
Essential medical treatments	Death or serious illness
Child support	Jail

Important bills are the ones that you should pay if at all possible, because failure to pay them would have serious consequences. Here are some examples.

The Bill	The Potential Consequence
Income taxes	Wage garnishment, loss of tax refund
Court judgments	Wage garnishment
Student loans	Wage garnishment, loss of tax refund
Loans secured by property	Repossession of property you want to keep
Auto insurance	Loss of license, fine
Medical insurance	Catastrophic medical bills

Nonessential bills include debts that aren't secured by property. Failure to pay these debts could have serious repercussions for your credit score and might eventually result in lawsuits and judgments. But skipping the payments listed next won't put you out on the street.

Nonessential Bills

Credit cards
Department store cards
Gas cards
Medical bills
Legal bills
Personal loans
Loans from friends or family members

You might have other bills not mentioned here; use your best judgment to categorize them.

After you have your list, go back and add two more columns:

- The monthly payment you typically make

- The minimum monthly payment you need to make to stay current

The minimum for most "friends and family" loans, by the way, is zero—unless you borrowed from your Uncle Tony, and his last name is Soprano.

Task 2: Match Your Resources to Your Bills and Debts

Look at the first two categories of savings that you identified in step 1—the easy stuff to cut and the harder stuff—and then add those to your monthly net income (what you get in your paycheck after all the taxes and other deductions have been taken). Now compare that income to your first two priorities—essential bills and important bills. Can you cover the minimums required?

If not, see whether you can trim the cost of some of these bills. Many people find they can cut back what they spend on utilities or groceries, for example. If you're still straining, consider deeper cuts, like switching to a cheaper child-care option or taking in a roommate.

If that's not enough, you might have some options before opting for the last-ditch cost-cutting measures. It's frequently possible, for example, to get forbearance on your student loans or negotiate payment plans with the IRS. The first you can do yourself, just by talking to your lender; for IRS help, you're probably best off using a tax pro. Even child support can be reduced if you prove to the court that your financial situation has worsened, but this can take awhile and might require a lawyer's help.

Other possibilities: You might take that second job we talked about earlier. You could increase your paycheck by eliminating or reducing 401(k) contributions temporarily or, if you get a tax refund, by reducing your with-holding.

If you still can't pay for the essential and the important, you'll probably need to take some last-resort action, such as selling a house if you own one or renting cheaper digs. You'll also need to consult a bankruptcy attorney about wiping out any nonessential debts, because those obviously aren't going to get paid.

If you have your bases covered and have money left over, however, check to see if you can pay the minimums on your nonessential bills. If you can pay at least that much, you're ready for the next task.

Task 3: Figuring Out a Repayment Plan

Your mission: To see if you can pay off those nonessential debts, other than friends and family loans, in *five years*.

Why that particular time period?

Because that's the standard generally used in bankruptcy court. If you have enough income and assets to pay most or all your bills within that time frame, a judge probably wouldn't let you pursue a Chapter 7 bankruptcy.

You can find debt-reduction calculators on the Internet, at sites such as Bankrate.com and CreditCards.com. With these, you can experiment to see how long it might take you to pay off your unsecured debts. Similar tools are available in personal finance software, such as Quicken and Mint. Don't include your mortgage, student loans, or any other "essential" or "important" bills we covered in the previous task; you're just trying to design a plan for those nonessential debts.

First, see how much progress you can make with the increased income you identified; then add in the lump sums you've estimated that you could raise by selling stuff. Finally, check out how fast you could get out of debt if you took some of those last-ditch options.

You also could consider—carefully—using a home equity loan or line of credit to pay off your cards, if you have substantial equity and can find a willing lender. But do so only if you can commit to the following:

- Not using your credit cards to pile up more debt. (For most people, this will mean not using cards at all until the home equity borrowing is paid back.)

- Not borrowing more than 80 percent of your home equity (and preferably less) when your mortgage and home equity borrow-ing is combined. Home equity can be an important source of emergency funds that you don't want to squander. (Some lend-ers won't let you borrow that much, anyway. If home prices are declining in your area, you may have to shop hard to find a lender willing to let you borrow more than 60 percent or less of a home's worth.)

- Paying off the debt in the same three- to five-year period. In other words, don't use the home equity loan as an excuse to stretch out your debt.

Remember: If you don't commit to these steps, you'll ultimately just drive yourself deeper into debt.

In the best-case scenario, you'd be able to retire your credit card and other unsecured debt in less than five years without too much strain. If you still have good credit scores, you might even convince your lenders—just by asking—to lower your interest rate so that you can get the debt paid off faster. Credit card companies are often eager to give their best customers a break rather than risk losing them to competitors. If not, good credit scores typically mean other companies want your business; you may transfer your balances to other cards at lower rates. Check CreditCards.com, CardRatings.com, NerdWallet, and LowCards.com for current offers.

Of course, that particular door might be closed to you if you've already fallen behind on your payments. Late payments to even one of your creditors can cause your scores to fall to the point that other issuers won't want to take a chance on you. You won't get the low balance-transfer rates they offer to people with better scores, and you may not persuade them to grant you a new account, period. All this can make it that much harder to try to get your head above water.

If things are bad when you're just late with a few payments, you can imagine how lenders—and your credit scores—react when an account is unpaid for so long that the original creditor "charges off" the account. A charge-off is an accounting term that means the lender has given up hope of collecting. Accounts are typically charged off if they're unpaid for six months. Although some creditors then turn the account over to their internal collections departments, others sell the account for pennies on the dollar to outside collection firms.

Interestingly, it's the charge-off itself that does the most damage to your score. Collection actions are serious, as well, but what matters most is what the original creditor says about your account—and a charge-off is pretty much the worst thing the creditor can say.

If you're in this situation, consult the books I recommended at the beginning of this chapter for a detailed summary of your rights as well as the best strategies for negotiating with collection agencies. The fine points of dealing with collectors are well beyond the scope of this book.

But, as far as your credit score is concerned, keep these points in mind:

- Although late payments can hurt a credit score, a charge-off is even worse. If at all possible, try to avoid letting an account lapse for so long that it's charged off.

- If an account has not yet been charged off, try to pay the balance in full either at once or over time. Settling the account with the original creditor for less than you owe can hurt your credit score. (Settlements on collection accounts typically don't have as negative an effect; see the next chapter for details.)

- If an account has been sent to collections, you'll have the most leverage to negotiate if you can pay a lump sum. But even if you have to make payments, try to negotiate to have the collection action deleted from your credit report if at all possible. Although having the collection deleted won't erase the negative marks from your file—the most damaging mark is the charge-off, which the original creditor typically won't drop— getting rid of the collection notation often helps your score.

What if you can't find a way to get all your unsecured debts paid off, or you're just not sure if your plan will work? You essentially have two options: credit counseling or bankruptcy. Read on for what you need to know about each.

The Real Scoop on Credit Counseling

For years we saw the ads on television, the radio, and the Internet promising to "lower your interest rates," "reduce your monthly payments," "end collection calls," and "get you on the road to financial freedom."

Sometimes credit counseling agencies delivered on their promises. Other times, consumers wound up much worse off. Just read what Jeff in Cincinnati went through:

"A little over five years ago, I contacted AmeriDebt to see if they could lower the interest rates on my credit cards. Within 30 minutes, I had received a callback from a representative from AmeriDebt stating that they had lowered the rates on my credit cards. I was amazed at the speed in which they had done this. I started paying them $500 a month, and they were to disburse the funds to my creditors. The problem was they never paid my creditors. [After five months], they had $2,500 of my money that the creditors should have received. This sent my credit into a tailspin. I was not in trouble with my creditors and had never missed a payment of any kind until I started dealing with [this company]. The credit card companies were calling, and they stated that they had no record of AmeriDebt working on my behalf. Bottom line: My credit was now ruined. I went from a 750 Beacon score to a 520 within four months. I paid everyone off immediately, and it has taken almost five years to get my credit score to just below 700. The funny part is that AmeriDebt decided to finally pay out that $2,500 to my creditors after I [had] already paid them off."

AmeriDebt insisted that it helped hundreds of thousands of consumers pay their bills and avoid bankruptcy. It continued insisting, in fact, right up until the Federal Trade Commission (FTC) sued the company in 2003. The FTC said AmeriDebt lied to its customers about the fees it charged and the services it offered, leaving many of them worse off.

What's more, regulators said, AmeriDebt posed as a nonprofit company while actually funneling money to a for-profit arm.

AmeriDebt responded by closing its doors to new customers—but sending them to another heavily advertised credit counselor making similar claims of quick-and-easy solutions to debt problems.

Credit counseling used to be a sleepy field dominated by the National Foundation for Credit Counseling, a truly nonprofit organization funded in large part by contributions from banks and credit card companies. Its mission was to negotiate lower interest rates and payments for cash-strapped consumers so that they could avoid bankruptcy. The lender receiving these payments would return a portion of each check—a contribution known as "fair share"—to the credit-counseling agency to fund its operations.

As consumer debt spiraled in the 1990s, however, a new breed of credit counselor emerged, eager to get a piece of those lender contributions. To boost market share, these new counselors started going after customers who were perfectly able to make their payments but who just wanted a lower interest rate.

Disgusted, the major creditors started dropping their "fair share" contributions, making it tougher for the older agencies to make ends meet. Instead of supporting legitimate counselors, some credit card companies even tried to steer consumers away from counseling, telling them erroneously that such help was as bad for their credit as bankruptcy.

But that wasn't the worst of it. Many of the new credit counselors kept the first month's contributions or charged other fat, hidden fees. Some failed to pass along consumers' contributions at all, causing multiple late payments that devastated scores. Former employees of such firms told Congress that they were forced to use fake names and employ high-pressure "boiler-room" tactics to sign up new customers. The emphasis was on collecting fees—not providing counseling or offering education that might help consumers understand how to avoid debt in the future.

Finally, things got so bad that the IRS decided to act. The federal tax agency began auditing dozens of credit counselors and eventually revoked the tax-exempt status of about half the credit counseling industry.

"Over a period of years, tax-exempt credit counseling became a big business dominated by bad actors," the IRS's then-Commissioner Mark W. Everson said in a press release. "Our examinations substantiated that these organizations have not been operating for the public good and don't deserve tax-exempt status. They have poisoned an entire sector of the charitable community."

The IRS's move helped weed out some of the worst offenders, but you still need to be cautious if you're considering getting help.

Keep in mind that credit counseling is not a good option if you're current on your bills and can pay more than the minimums. As I explained in Chapter 5, "Credit-Scoring Myths," credit counseling itself won't hurt your credit score, but the reactions of some of your lenders might.

If you're already struggling, here are some of the things you need to consider before signing up with a credit counselor:

- **Is it accredited?** You'll want a counselor affiliated with the National Foundation for Credit Counseling or the Financial Counseling Association of America (formerly the Association of Independent Consumer Credit Counseling Agencies). You can find affiliated agencies at www.nfcc.org or www.aiccca. org, respectively.

- **What do regulators say about it?** At a minimum, make two calls: one to your local Better Business Bureau and one to your state attorney general's office. Ask how many complaints have been made about the agency, and determine whether any regulatory actions are pending against them.

- **What does the agency say about its services?** Avoid an outfit that says credit counseling will have no negative impact on your credit or one that promises to settle your debts for less than you owe without affecting your credit. Such unrealistic promises are a clear sign that you're not dealing with a legitimate operator.

- **What fees are involved?** Legitimate credit counselors have had to raise their fees in recent years, but if you're paying much more than $50 to set up your plan, you're probably paying too much.

- **When and how much will creditors get paid?** You know that missing or late payments can devastate your credit score. Make sure the counselor tells you, preferably in writing, how much of each monthly payment you make will go directly to your creditors and when the payments will arrive.

It's possible that after all this investigation, you'll discover that a credit counselor's debt management plan won't work. If your credit counselor crunches the numbers and discovers the agency can't help you pay off your bills within five years, you'll probably be told to "explore other legal options." That's code for: Talk to a bankruptcy attorney.

You might want to do that anyway, just to get more information about your options before you decide on a plan. Such a consultation is particularly important if your debts are overwhelming and you have equity in a home. States treat this equity differently, with some protecting all or most of it in bankruptcy court and others figuring it's up for grabs. If you can't protect your equity, it might be worth getting a home equity loan to pay off your debts, assuming you have enough equity available.

After you've heard what both the credit counselor and the bankruptcy attorney have to say, you can weigh all the information you've been given and make a choice.

Debt Settlement: A Risky Option

As bogus credit counselors have been shut down, a new breed of firms promising debt deliverance has taken over airwaves and the Internet. They essentially promise to settle your debts for pennies on the dollar.

Although the schemes vary somewhat, the basic idea is that you stop paying your bills and instead save up the cash that the firm will then use to negotiate a settlement of your debts. Failing to pay your bills on time will, of course, trash your credit scores, and settlements, especially with your original creditors, can do additional damage.

The worst of these firms make unrealistic promises, assure you your credit won't be harmed, and disappear after taking thousands of your dollars. Even working with a legitimate firm can lead to lawsuits and wage garnishment as creditors retaliate.

In 2010, the Federal Trade Commission forbade debt settlement firms from charging upfront fees for their services. The FTC also implemented new rules requiring more disclosure and more safeguards for any funds customers put aside to pay their bills. There are still plenty of firms trying to skirt these new regulations, though, so it's still buyer beware.

Debt settlement makes little sense for people who can successfully file a Chapter 7 bankruptcy (details on that later) to erase most unsecured debts. If you can't pay your bills, after all, you're financially much better off eliminating the debt entirely and saving yourself the debt-settlement firm's fees and the risk of lawsuits.

If you can't file for Chapter 7 and would face a five-year Chapter 13 repayment plan instead, debt settlement might be an option. Debt settlement could have you free of your bills in two to three years. But you'll want to choose your company carefully.

The Federal Trade Commission has said legitimate debt-settlement companies should

- Not guarantee results.

- Not accept clients who have the means to pay their bills.

- Have written policies and procedures about their debt-settlement program.

- Be a member of the Better Business Bureau.

- Have a customer dispute-resolution and review process.

- Have in-house legal counsel with significant experience in credit industry compliance.

- Handle clients in-house, never referring them to a third party.

- Offer full disclosure of all program fees and costs before the start of a debt settlement program.

- Inform customers that the IRS classifies any forgiven debt above $600 as income that can be taxed.

- Require prospective clients to commit to saving money on their own to fund settlements. This money shouldn't be handled or escrowed by the debt settlement firm because of the risk of embezzlement and fraud.

- Negotiate on an ongoing basis with creditors and present all settlement offers to the customer for his exclusive approval.

Credit expert Gerri Detweiler of Credit.com says you should avoid any company that assures you that

- It can settle debt without hurting your credit.

- You can't be sued. (You can!)

- It can stop creditors from calling you. (It can request that they stop but can't prevent them from ignoring this request.)

- It can predict how much you'll save or exactly how much the settlements will cost.

In addition, Detweiler says any of the following are also red flags:

- **Fees aren't based on performance or results**—Detweiler doesn't like companies that collect money up front or based on a percentage of your debt.

- **Counselors are paid on commission**—Detweiler believes this increases the chances counselors will lie to get you in the door.

- **No money-back guarantee**—You should have at least 30 days to change your mind and receive a refund of at least some of your fees if none of your debts are settled.

- **Inexperience**—Many companies have sprung into existence recently and have little experience successfully negotiating settlements.

Should You File for Bankruptcy?

In the fall of 2003, I asked MSN readers to share their bankruptcy stories: why they filed, how it has affected them, and whether they thought they made the right choice. I expected a few dozen replies.

I received more than 500 emails. I was stunned not only at the breadth of the response, but also the depth. Most were long, detailed missives that recounted financial catastrophes, such as lost jobs and huge medical bills, personal tragedies including the death of a spouse or a child, and a wide variety of human miscalculations: trusting the wrong business partner, marrying a secret gambler, or simply spending way more than they earned.

Most believed that filing bankruptcy was the right choice for them; although many admitted to mixed feelings. Here's just a small cross-section of their responses:

"I filed last year and released about…$40,000 in credit card debt. I researched and pondered the idea for quite awhile before actually doing it, but ultimately it provided me a fresh start. Now I am a regular, financially upstanding citizen, and I have learned my lesson…. Had I not been protected by bankruptcy laws, I would still be struggling."
—Erin in Honolulu

"I don't think bankruptcy is ever the 'right' decision, but I felt it was my only choice at the time. For me, it was embarrassing and humiliating….
It is now six years later, and I've done all I can to restore my credit by making sure all my bills are paid on time, and I pay all my debts as quickly as possible. The children are both now grown and on their own, I'm making twice the wages I was [at the time of the filing]… that doesn't make any difference. I still have trouble getting credit."
—Cathy in Montana

"I filed bankruptcy in 1998 and have gotten myself in trouble once again. Currently I'm about $3,000 in debt, which consists of cell phone bills and credit cards that started out with a limit of $300 or $500… all of which are probably in or close to being in collection."
—Leslie in Washington, DC

"We filed Chapter 7 in 1999 due to bills piling up as a result of [our busi-ness failing]. One year later, we applied and were approved for a credit card with a 13 percent interest rate. I also bought a new car at what I consider a somewhat outrageous rate of 16 percent and missed out on all the 0 percent financing offered after September 11. Basically, one can survive a bankruptcy as long as the pay history is kept up to date on all debts afterward."
—*Rob in Grand Prairie, Texas*

"It has been almost four years since I sat in an attorney's office, papers filled in ready to file for bankruptcy. I was a newly sober alcoholic wanting to make a fresh start in my new life.... I decided that filing for bankruptcy was a cop-out, and that it was unfair to the companies (small and large) that I had defaulted on. Since that day, I have [been making payments].... In April 2007, my record will be clear of all negative items, and I achieved this without filing bankruptcy."
—*Ken in Santa Rosa, California*

As you can see from these responses, people's experiences with bank-ruptcy can vary widely. Whether it's the right choice depends on the types of debt you owe and the amounts, your income and resources, and your ability to navigate the inevitable fallout, among other factors.

The Effects of Bankruptcy Reform

In 2005, after several years of trying, Congress finally succeeded in passing a bankruptcy reform act to make erasing debts more difficult for higher-income borrowers. These debtors would be subjected to a "means test" that was supposed to determine whether they could repay some of their debts.

The new legislation set off a stampede, as debtors rushed to file bank-ruptcy before the new limitations went into effect. By the end of the year, more than two million cases had been filed—a number that shattered all previous records.

Publicity about the new law led to a lot of misconceptions. Many people believed, erroneously, that bankruptcy had been eliminated as an option or that everyone who filed would be forced to repay at least some of what they owed.

In reality, the new means test applies only to filers whose incomes are above the median level for their area. Most people filing for bankruptcy have incomes below the median, so they aren't subjected to the means test. For them, the biggest impact of the reform is that filing for bankruptcy has become significantly more costly than in the past. A typical Chapter 7 may cost $1,200 or more in filing and attorney's fees, whereas a Chapter 13 bankruptcy can cost $3,000 and up.

Still, that didn't prevent bankruptcy filings from rising as the economy soured. Filings in 2008 topped one million—back to the same level that prompted lenders to begin lobbying for bankruptcy reform a decade earlier—and in 2010 consumer filings topped 1.5 million.

The Type of Bankruptcy That You File Matters

The majority of people who file for bankruptcy opt for Chapter 7, which wipes out most unsecured debts. (Unsecured debts are those that aren't linked to specific property, such as a car or a house. So your mortgage is a secured debt; your credit card bills are unsecured.)

Filing a Chapter 7 bankruptcy can mean you have to give up some of your assets (property or cash) to pay your creditors. In reality, most Chapter 7 filers aren't required to give up anything, either because they don't have any assets or because the property they have is "exempt" or protected from creditors. The exemptions vary by state, but they might include household furnishings, clothing, tools you need for work, retirement accounts, and some—or all—of the equity in your home.

If you want to keep property that isn't exempt, you can still file for bankruptcy, but you typically must choose Chapter 13. You also might be shunted into a Chapter 13 bankruptcy if your income is above the median for your area and the new bankruptcy reform means test shows that you can repay some of what you owe.

Chapter 13 requires debtors to come up with a five-year repayment plan. If they successfully complete their plan, they're allowed to keep their property while having any remaining debts erased. Unfortunately, most people fail to complete their Chapter 13 plans, and their cases are either dismissed, allowing creditors to resume collection activities, or converted to Chapter 7s.

A bankruptcy filing can make sense if any of the following apply:

- You can't pay back your unsecured debts, such as credit cards and medical bills, within five years.

- You don't have much equity in a home or vehicle or much other property to speak of.

- You *do* have considerable equity in a home or vehicle or other valuables that wouldn't be exempt in bankruptcy—jewels; family heirlooms; valuable artwork or collections; or stocks, bonds, and cash held outside a retirement plan—but you're willing to agree to a Chapter 13 repayment plan rather than a Chapter 7 liquidation.

Bankruptcy might not make sense if any of these apply:

- You could repay your debts within five years.

- Most of your debts are the kind that can't be wiped out. Debts that typically can't be erased include student loans, child support, and recent taxes. You might still decide to file so that you can free up more money for these debts, but the disadvantages of filing might overwhelm the advantages.

- You defrauded your creditors by hiding assets, say, or lying about your income or debts on a credit application.

- You recently ran up large debts buying luxuries, which can include vacations and entertainment. If you did so while you were clearly broke, that can constitute fraud. If you ran up the bills and then lost your job, you might be able to file for bankruptcy on other debts, but the luxury debts might not be wiped out.

- You want to file a Chapter 7 liquidation bankruptcy and received a discharge for a previous bankruptcy filing within the past eight years. (You can file for a Chapter 13 repayment plan bankruptcy at any time.)

- You're reluctant to leave a coborrower solely responsible for a debt. A bankruptcy filing can wipe out your legal obligation to repay a loan, but creditors can still go after a cosigner or joint borrower.

Making the decision to file isn't an easy one, and you'd be smart to get expert help to explore your options. Many bankruptcy attorneys offer a free initial consultation. For more information, a good book to read is *The New Bankruptcy: Will It Work for You?* by attorneys Leon Bayer and Stephen Elias (Nolo, 2015).

Should You Walk Away from Your Home?

Loose lending standards put many people into homes they ultimately couldn't afford. Others found themselves struggling to pay their mortgages after they lost their jobs. And still others decided to walk away from homes they could afford because their properties were worth less than what they owed. These so-called strategic defaults accounted for about one in three foreclosures in 2011.

People who voluntarily default often reason, probably correctly, that their credit scores may heal before property values do. Although property values have rebounded in many areas, they've been slow to recover in others. Seven years after the real estate recession began, prices had yet to return to their peaks in 40 of the 50 largest markets, according to a *Wall Street Journal* analysis of home sales data from Zillow. Meanwhile, as you learned in a previous chapter, someone with FICOs in the 680 range would recover her old scores in about three years, while someone with 780 FICOs could reattain her old scores in seven years or so.

Still, the decision to stop paying a mortgage is a difficult one for many people. As the recession worsened, many tried to get mortgage modifications or refinancings from their lenders, only to have their paperwork repeatedly lost or their applications rejected for bogus or trivial reasons. Some were approved for trial modifications—and then the lender moved forward with foreclosure anyway. (In one particularly tragic case, a couple's daughter and her grandparents were killed in a traffic accident. When the couple asked for more time to file their paperwork as they dealt with this horror, their bank responded by sending them a foreclosure notice.) Bankruptcy attorney Stephen Elias told me that many of his clients who originally insisted they had a moral obligation to pay their loans had that attitude beaten out of them by the indifference, avarice, or seeming incompetence of their lenders.

If your mortgage is problematic, your first step should be to contact a HUD-approved housing counselor (www.hud.gov) who can assess your situation and advise you about alternatives. You may qualify for help through a government-sponsored modification or refinance program, or you may work out a more affordable arrangement directly with your lender. Although some frustrated homeowners have said they couldn't get their banks' attention until they stopped paying their mortgages, you are not required to be behind on your payments to get help—and not paying your mortgage will have significant negative impacts on your credit scores.

If you can't get help, you should assess whether your mortgage is truly affordable. The federal government typically defines an affordable mortgage as one that consumes 31 percent of the borrower's gross income. In my view, a mortgage that eats up much more than 25 percent of your gross income may not be workable, because you may not have enough money left over to cover other important costs such as saving for retirement, building an emergency fund, and educating your children.

Too many people throw half or more of their incomes at a mortgage—a situation that is simply not sustainable in the long run. What's worse is when people raid their retirement funds to make their mortgage payments, draining their future nest eggs for a home they might ultimately lose anyway. Before you withdraw or borrow money from a retirement fund to pay a debt—any debt—you should talk to a bankruptcy attorney about the legal and financial repercussions of what you're doing.

If you know you can't afford your mortgage, you have several options:

- **A short sale**—If the lender agrees, you may be able to sell your home for less than what you owe. Although a typical short sale has the same impact on your credit scores as a foreclosure, you should qualify for another mortgage after two years, versus a wait of up to seven years after a foreclosure. Always have your own attorney review any short sale agreement, however. Lenders have been known to pursue borrowers for unpaid mortgage amounts, even after agreeing to a short sale. You'll want clear language in the agreement that you're no longer on the hook for this debt.

- **Deed-in-lieu of foreclosure**—You're essentially handing the keys over to the bank rather than waiting to go through the formal foreclosure process, which would otherwise take months if not years. Your credit scores will still suffer; although you may qualify for another mortgage sooner, as with a short sale. Again, try to make sure you can't be pursued for the leftover debt.

- **Foreclosure**—The formal foreclosure process varies by state—some go through the courts; some don't. Some states don't allow lenders to pursue borrowers for unpaid debt after a foreclosure, while some do. The details vary enough that you'll want to research your particular state's laws and discuss your situation with a bankruptcy attorney or other lawyer familiar with the credit laws—and lender practices—of your state. Foreclosure has one big advantage over a short sale or deed-in-lieu in that it takes longer. Why is that a good thing? Because you can continue living in your home, rent free, while the process grinds on. If you save up the money you would otherwise commit to mortgage payments, you'll have a stash that can help you in your post-foreclosure life—by making a big deposit that could convince a reluctant landlord to rent to you, for example.

Before you choose any of these options, you should read attorney Elias's book *The Foreclosure Survival Guide: Keep Your House or Walk Away with Money in Your Pocket*" (Nolo Press, 2009; co-authored with Amy Loftsgordon) and discuss your situation with a qualified attorney.

A new twist on the crisis has begun to emerge in recent years, as much higher payments kicked in on home equity lines of credit taken out at the market peak. These lines of credit typically require only interest payments in the initial 10 years, but after that time switch to a payment that includes principal as well as interest.

Homeowners with sufficient equity, incomes, and credit scores may be able to qualify for a new home equity line that puts off the day of reckoning. Another option might be a "cash out" refinance of their primary mortgage to pay off the line and essentially add its balance to the first mortgage.

Those who aren't in a good position to get another loan should contact their lenders to see if there is a workable solution. To lower payments, some banks have been willing to extend the payback period or defer interest until the end of the loan.

Step 3: Choose Your Path and Take Action

When faced with unappealing choices, it's natural to procrastinate. But after you've assessed your situation, gathered the relevant information, and sought expert help, the path you need to take should be pretty clear.

Option 1: The Pay-Off Plan

If you can pay off your unsecured debts without help or with the help of home equity borrowing, you're ready to take the first step: cutting up your credit cards. "What?" you might be saying. "Cut up my cards? How can I live without my cards?" News flash: People do it all the time.

You can't get out of debt if you keep digging. And if you have easy access to your cards, you'll keep using them. Your credit cards—at least most of them—need to be off limits until you're debt free. Debit cards with

Visa or MasterCard logos are accepted at most places that take credit cards; the difference is that the money comes directly out of your checking account, so it's much tougher to overspend.

The big risk with debit cards is fraud. If a criminal gets hold of your account number, she can drain your bank account—and then you'll have to wait to get your money back. The computer-chip technology that banks are finally adopting will help curb fraud, but you're still at risk as long as your card has a magnetic stripe on the back because those are easily compromised. If you're not comfortable using your debit card—and that's a reasonable attitude—then consider using a credit card that currently has no balance for purchases you can't make with cash. The key is *paying this card in full every month*. If you can't do that, then use cash.

You don't need to actually close your credit card accounts, which could potentially hurt your score, unless you really have an uncontrollable spending issue.

Next, set up an automatic payment plan as outlined earlier to pay off your debts. The order in which you pay them depends on your particular situation. If you have an account that's close to being charged off, for example, you'll probably want to catch up with that one right away while paying the minimums on your other debts. If you're not behind, you could start paying down the account that's closest to its limit, or the one that's charging the highest nondeductible interest rate. After the first debt is retired, redirect the biggest payment to the next-highest-rate—or closest-to-the-limit—debt. Continue this pattern until all the debts are retired.

Option 2: Credit Counseling

If you decide you need a credit counselor's aid, make the appointment to get started on a debt management plan. Every day you delay is costing you more in interest and putting off the moment when you'll be debt free.

Understand that paying off your debts will be a long-term commitment, and that living on the tight budget necessary may be frustrating. If you need motivation to keep going, consider joining the message boards of one of the frugality-oriented Web sites to get support and keep your spirits up.

Option 3: Debt Settlement

Before you agree to debt settlement, make sure you've consulted a legitimate credit counselor and a bankruptcy attorney so that you understand your other options. Thoroughly research the debt-settlement firm before agreeing to its services. Commit to setting aside the money you'll need for settlements—many people drop out of debt settlement after just a few months because it's too tempting to spend the money on other things.

Option 4: Bankruptcy

If bankruptcy is the best of bad options, then file. The bankruptcy laws were designed to give people a fresh start; and if you've done your best to find money to pay your bills and failed, you shouldn't shun this option.

7

Rebuilding Your Score
After a Credit Disaster

So you've weathered the financial storm. Now what do you do about the mess that was left behind?

Your credit file might be littered with delinquencies, collection actions, repossessions, or even bankruptcy. You might worry that these mistakes will haunt you forever, or at least make getting credit terribly difficult and expensive.

Some people are so frustrated with their bad credit that they simply give up. Maureen in Cleveland wrote me about her daughter and son-in-law, who were turned down for several loans after filing bankruptcy. Humiliated, they vowed never to approach another lender:

> *"They've given up on their dream of owning their own house someday," Maureen wrote. "I know they could do something about their credit if they would just try."*

Contrast their attitude with that of Chance, an Indiana loan officer who filed for Chapter 7 bankruptcy five years earlier at age 27:

"Today I have a 697 middle score, and I can get a loan for anything I want to," Chance wrote. "I own a home and two rental properties, have a brand new auto and motorcycle…. Being in the mortgage industry, I knew I could overcome the bankruptcy, because I knew how the credit system worked."

Lenders' willingness to give people a second chance waxes and wanes along with the economy. In bad economic times, those with bad credit usually find it harder to get the accounts and loans they need to rebuild their credit. But there will still be ways to get started.

Credit-scoring formulas care more about what you've done recently than what you've done in the past, so making the right moves now can set you on the path to good credit.

You won't be able to erase your mistakes overnight. However, most people with past credit problems can achieve a substantial boost in their credit scores within a couple years. By the time the last negative item drops off your credit report—after seven years for most black marks, or up to ten for a Chapter 7 bankruptcy—you could have a credit score that's actually better than average.

Rehabilitating a Troubled Account

If you've fallen behind on a credit card or loan but can now catch up and make your payments on time, you may be in luck: Some lenders will help you "rehabilitate" your account.

This is particularly true for student loans. Many lenders will erase negative marks from your credit reports after you've made 12 months of on-time payments.

Some credit card issuers offer this option, too; although they may limit it to customers who've only been late once in the past 12 or 24 months. Again, you need to make a series of on-time payments before the delinquency is erased.

It can't hurt to ask your creditors if they offer this option. The worst they can say is no.

Part I: Credit Report Repair

Many people who have credit problems are terrified at the prospect of looking at their credit report. It's the same dread they might have felt as children about a bad report card, only amplified by their adult knowledge of how destructive poor credit can be.

In actuality, your report might be better than you think. Some of the problems you are worried about might never have been reported to the credit bureaus, or they might have less of an effect than you fear.

However, your credit file might be a bit of a nightmare, with every slip-up documented in black and white. Your report might even make your problems look worse than they actually were. It's not uncommon to have two or more collections reported for the same debt, for example, or for other errors to creep in that can hammer your credit score.

You might, for example, be the victim of an unscrupulous collection agency that has illegally "re-aged" a debt—in other words, reported the account to the credit bureaus in a way that makes your mistake look more recent than it actually is. Beth in Los Angeles wrote about just such a scofflaw:

"My husband and I had a dispute with a cable company over a box that they never gave us, but that they claimed we owed $200 for when we closed the account before we moved. To make a long story short, the item ended up on our credit report as a collection account.

"We waited anxiously for that to roll off of our report. At the six-year, two-month mark, another collection agency called us. They said they had bought the account, and that the seven-year 'clock' started again when they bought it. They said unless we paid them, they would report it as a new debt and it would remain on our credit report for seven more years."

The good news is that you're not helpless. There are steps you can take to clean up your credit, chase off mistakes, fight back against illegal tactics, and even—perhaps—scoot some of those bad marks off your report without having to wait for the usual seven- or ten-year period to expire.

Scrutinize Your Report for Serious Errors

Your first move is to get copies of your credit reports from all three bureaus, using the addresses or Web sites listed in Chapter 4, "Improving Your Score—The Right Way." Make sure you get three separate reports, rather than a "3-in-1" or "tri-merged" report that combines information from the three bureaus. Although these merged reports are helpful to lenders, they might not include all the information that's included in each bureau's files.

Follow the steps listed in Chapter 4 for reviewing your report, noting any problems for dispute with the respective credit bureaus. Look especially for the following:

- Delinquencies that are older than seven years, or accounts listed as delinquent that don't include the date of delinquency

- Bankruptcies that are older than ten years or that aren't listed by the specific chapter

- Judgments or paid liens older than seven years

- Paid-off debts listed as unpaid

- Accounts that were wiped out by a bankruptcy filing still listed as "past due" instead of as "included in bankruptcy"

- More than one collection account for the same debt

- Collection accounts that don't show the date that the original account went delinquent

- Any accounts, delinquencies, collections, and so on that aren't yours

When it's time to actually dispute the errors you find, you have a choice about whether to make your beefs online or by snail mail. Some credit repair veterans prefer to use the online dispute process that's available when you get your reports via the Web; they believe there's less likelihood of their disputes getting "lost" because the electronic process typically dumps their complaints directly into the bureaus' computer systems. If you do opt for online disputes, make printouts of every form you fill out and every response you get. Doing so establishes the kind of paper trail that can be incredibly helpful if you run into problems.

The need for a paper trail is why others insist that all communication with bureaus, creditors, and especially collection agencies should be in writing and sent certified mail, return receipt requested. Keep the little green cards you get back, along with copies of the letters and any documentation you might submit. Because you're probably new to the credit repair process, you might want to start out doing things the old-fashioned way and switch to the electronic process only when you become more comfortable with the system.

Know Your Rights

Before you dispute anything, though, you need to know your rights under the Fair Credit Reporting Act. They are as follows:

- **The right to have your dispute investigated**—The bureaus must investigate your dispute, usually within 30 days, by contacting the creditor, collection agency, or other "information provider" that supplied the data in question. Any information provider contacted in this way must launch its own investigation and report its results back to the bureau. The term "investigation" is a bit of a misnomer, though. Most of the process is highly automated, with the bureaus' computers querying the creditors' computers. Consumer advocates have long complained that the system bears little resemblance to a meaningful review of questionable data. The bureaus' recent settlements with regulators offer hope that this will change, and that you'll get a human being involved to help you resolve disputes. You still should expect a fight to get your record cleared, though. Also, there's a major exception to the 30-day rule. If the credit bureaus decide your dispute is "frivolous," they might tell you so and refuse to investigate. This tends to happen if you repeatedly demand investigations of information that's already been verified. Although this can prevent scam artists from taking advantage of the system, it can be frustrating for people who are dealing with a creditor that refuses to correct its errors.

- **The right to have erroneous information corrected**—If the provider says the information is indeed inaccurate, it is required to notify not just the bureau that originally contacted it, but all the other major credit bureaus, too, so that the error can be fixed or the item deleted. If the provider can't verify the information, the information must be deleted from your credit report.

    The bureaus can, however, reinsert the deleted information or undo the correction later if the provider verifies that the original item was in fact complete and correct. This exception can frustrate the heck out of consumers who think they have their reports cleaned up, only to see the bad information pop up again after a few months.

- **The right to a written response**—After completing its investigation, the bureau must give you a written report of its findings and a free copy of your credit report if the investigation changed anything on your file. Furthermore, if the bureau later restores the information that was deleted or changed, it must notify you in writing and provide you with the name, address, and phone number of the information provider.

- **The right to have a statement included in your file**—If the dispute doesn't resolve the way you want, you are entitled to a 100-word statement inserted into your credit report explaining your side of the story. As you read earlier in this book, though, these statements have no effect on a credit score. Therefore, even though you have this right, you're much better off pursuing other avenues that can actually make a difference if you're being stymied by a recalcitrant creditor.

- **The right to sue**—If a creditor or collection agency violates these rights—by continuing to report inaccurate, unsubstantiated information, for example, or failing to respond to your dispute—you can sue the creditor or agency in state or federal court. Some people have even pursued these claims successfully in small claims court. Hopefully, your problems can be resolved without a judge's involvement. But you might need the threat of a lawsuit, and perhaps legal representation to back it up, if you're dealing with a particularly troublesome creditor or unresponsive credit bureau.

Organize Your Attack

At this point, you should divide the errors you've discovered into two groups. The first group includes unpaid debts that actually belong to you (as opposed to debts that you didn't incur or that belong to someone else), including any debt you suspect was illegally re-aged, and any collection accounts (whether they're legitimately yours or not). All the other errors you discover— accounts that aren't yours, old delinquencies on paid-up accounts, debts that were included in bankruptcy but aren't listed that way, and so on— should be included in the second group.

You can get started disputing the items in that second group right away. Include copies of any documentation you have that supports your assertion with your letters to the credit bureaus. (Never send originals.) After you've notified the credit bureaus, follow up by sending a letter (certified, return receipt requested) to the creditor that supplied the erroneous information.

Now all the creditors and the bureaus are on notice that there's a problem. Failure to act on their part would be a violation of federal fair credit reporting rules and grounds enough for a lawsuit—again, if it comes to that.

In many cases, the creditors and bureaus will correct legitimate errors. However, you'll still need to monitor your credit reports to make sure the bad information doesn't pop up again in the future. If that happens, the paperwork you've kept—including notification that the bureaus give you about the changes they've made—might help you get the errors removed more quickly.

If the creditor or other information provider insists that its information is accurate, however, you might need to dispute the information with them again—or you might just want to head straight to a lawyer. Sometimes a firmly worded missive on an attorney's letterhead is all it takes to get a creditor to see the error of its ways. If not, there's always a lawsuit. The National Association of Consumer Advocates at www.naca.net can provide referrals to attorneys.

What You Need to Know About Unpaid Debts and Collections

Now let's return to that first group of errors you identified—the ones dealing with collection accounts and valid, unpaid debts. These were segregated, because different rules apply.

When it comes to collections, you have another important right as outlined in the Fair Debt Collection Practices Act:

- **The right to have a collection account "validated"**—This process, as outlined in the FDCPA, is quite different from the "verification" process referred to previously. When a credit bureau asks a creditor to "verify" information, the investigation that follows can be pretty cursory. With verification, the creditor reviews its records and any information supplied by the consumer and then decides whether it (the creditor) was right or wrong.

  When a collection agency is asked to validate a debt, by contrast, the process can get pretty involved. The collector must *prove* that the debt is your responsibility and that it has the legal right to collect it from you. Furthermore, the collector has to cease all collection activity until it provides this evidence to you. If the agency can't validate the debt, it must end its attempts to collect on the debt and stop reporting the collections account to the credit bureaus.

Note that your right to validation applies specifically to collection agencies, not to the original creditor. Collection agency records are presumed to be less reliable than those kept by the original creditors. Collectors are often guilty of going after the wrong people or misstating the amounts owed; the validation process is meant to protect consumers from those practices.

To validate a debt, the collector needs to present documentation—obtained from the original creditor—proving that you do indeed owe the money.

Validation can be a powerful weapon in your fight to clean up collection actions on your credit report. Many times collectors don't have the documentation required, especially if the debt has been passed around from one collection agency to another, as often happens. Frequently, they have little more than a computer printout to back up their claims, and the Federal Trade Commission has made it clear that such a "mere itemization" isn't sufficient proof to constitute a validation of a debt.

The validation process can not only help you eliminate collection accounts that don't belong to you, but it might also help you get rid of some that actually do.

That last statement might surprise you, particularly if you've heard the credit bureau company line that you can't legally remove true, negative information from your credit report. I admit that I used to parrot that line myself, usually when trying to warn people away from the many scam artists who promise to erase all the bad information on your credit report in exchange for a fat fee.

I've since learned that sometimes—not always, but sometimes—you *can* get accurate information removed from your file, especially if it has to do with an old collection account.

Now, the bureaus and Fair Isaac will tell you that this isn't "playing fair"—that the integrity of the credit system depends on credit reports reflecting the most complete picture possible, including all available negative and positive information.

Unfortunately, the bureaus are still allowing far too much erroneous data to seep into their system, and that's hurting consumers. The credit-reporting process is still weighted heavily in favor of lenders and collectors.

That steams Jim Stephenson, a realtor in Branson, Missouri, who has watched several of his clients struggle with inaccurate credit information:

"If I'm a subscriber [to the credit bureaus], all I need is your Social Security number and I can tell them anything derogatory about you I want. Without question or hesitation, this info goes onto your credit file. It can be extremely difficult to prove a negative. How do you prove that you don't owe me money?" Jim wrote. "Time and again I have

witnessed firsthand the inability of a client to have misinformation
that is irrefutably not my client's debt removed without a
protracted and costly fight. Why is this? It's because
the burden of proof is on the accused, not the accuser."

The issue of re-aging can be particularly troublesome. The seven-year limit on reporting most negative items was designed to give consumers some protection against relentless creditors. In effect, lawmakers were trying to prevent collection agencies from creating a sort of perpetual debtors' prison for people who had made mistakes. Congress even strengthened the law in the mid-1990s to prevent collectors from endlessly extending the seven-year time period just by passing an account from one agency to the next (as Beth's collection agency was threatening to do). Instead of using the "date of last activity," as was common before 1997, the seven-year clock now starts 180 days after the account first became delinquent.

To get around the limit, some collection agencies are now simply flouting the law and pretending an old debt is a new one. I've received numerous letters from consumers who had long-forgotten delinquent accounts suddenly pop back up on their credit reports with a new and phony date. One of the largest collection agencies, NCO Financial Systems, agreed in early 2004 to settle a lawsuit with a group of borrowers over this issue.

Unfortunately, the type of collector that would actually post false information to a credit bureau file might not be the type that will back down in the face of a validation demand or a credit bureau investigation. You'll still need to make the validation demand, of course, and follow up with a credit bureau dispute if you don't get the response you want. But it might take a lawsuit to get the falsely incriminating information out of your file.

There's another issue. Plenty of consumers are like Beth and Dave in Chapter 6, "Coping with a Credit Crisis," in that they let spats with merchants get out of hand and wind up with collections on their reports. These collections—even for relatively small amounts—can have an outsized effect on a credit score. The thinner or younger your credit file, the worse a collection can hurt. Although mortgage lenders tend to ignore these small accounts, credit-scoring formulas might not. Getting rid of collections can create a more accurate picture of your credit habits.

It's also not uncommon to have two, three, or even more collection accounts reported for the same debt. That amplifies the damage to your credit score and reflects the collection industry's practice of selling and reselling the same debt to different companies. Weeding out some of these extraneous collection accounts provides a more accurate picture of your credit situation.

Besides, I'm going to assume that if you care enough about your credit to read this book and spend the time necessary to clean up your credit report, you're demonstrating the kind of dedication and responsibility that should make you a good credit risk in the future.

You shouldn't assume, however, that you can get every piece of negative information removed—far from it. The more recent the negative mark, the less likely you'll get it to budge. Your chances of success will improve as the "sin" gets older.

You also have no guarantee that getting rid of a collection action will help your score much, if at all. The scoring formula generally weighs what the original creditor had to say about you more heavily than what any subsequent collector reports. In other words, delinquencies and charge-offs reported by the original creditor can still hurt your score even if the subsequent collections disappear.

Okay, that's enough background. If you're trying to get rid of a collection action, credit repair veterans suggest first disputing it as "not mine," rather than starting off with a validation demand.

Sometimes, the collection agency simply won't bother to verify the account, particularly if it's old or small. If that's the case, the collection will be dropped from your report—no muss, no fuss.

If the credit bureau verifies the account, go directly to the collection agency and demand validation. You can find sample letters at Web sites such as CreditBoards.com or CreditInfoCenter.com. Essentially, you need to tell the collection agency that under the Fair Debt Collection Practices Act, it must prove that you owe this debt. Demand copies of documents such as the signed account agreement that created the debt and the agreement with the original creditor that gives the agency the right to try to collect the debt.

If the collector fails to respond or can't provide sufficient evidence that you owe the debt, it's supposed to remove the collection from your report. If that doesn't happen, you can bring the matter to the attention of the credit bureaus and ask for an investigation. Make sure you make it clear to the bureaus that this is not a repeat of your earlier request; provide the evidence that you asked for validation, and let them know that the collector didn't comply.

If the account doesn't disappear at this point, you have both the bureaus and the collection agency on the hook for credit-reporting violations and potentially could pursue a lawsuit.

What You Need to Know About Statutes of Limitations

Before we go any further down this path, however, you need to know about one more factor that will affect your credit repair efforts: statutes of limitations.

You already know that credit bureaus have a limited time (seven to ten years) in which they can report negative information. The statutes of limitations I'm talking about, however, curb the amount of time that a creditor can sue you over a debt.

Statutes of limitations vary widely by state and might depend on the type of debt involved. In Alaska, for example, creditors can't sue you after 3 years have passed since the delinquency. In Kentucky, the statute is 15 years for written contracts, and 5 for oral contracts. Depending on the state, open-ended contracts—such as credit cards—might be considered a written contract, an oral contract, or have a different statute of limitations altogether.

Statutes of Limitations for the 50 States (and the District of Columbia)

State	Statute	Written Contract	Oral Contract	Injury	Property Damage
Alabama	Ala. Code § 6-2-2 et seq. *	6	6	2	6
Alaska	Alaska Stat. § 09.10.010 et seq.	3	3	2	6 (real property); 2 (personal property)
Arizona	Ariz. Rev. Stat. Ann. § 12-541 et seq.	6	3	2	2
Arkansas	Ark. Code Ann. § 16-56-101 et seq.	5	3	3	3
California	Cal. Civ. Proc. Code § 312 et seq.	4	2	2	3
Colorado	Colo. Rev. Stat. § 13-80-102 et seq.	3 (6 most debts; rent) (2 tortious breach	3 (6 short-term debt/rent) (2 tortious breach)	2	2
Connecticut	Conn. Gen. Stat. Ann. § 52-575 et seq.	6	3	2	2
Delaware	Del. Code Ann. tit. 10, § 8101 et seq.	3	3	2	2
District of Columbia	D.C. Code § 12-301 et seq.	3	3	3	3
Florida	Fla. Stat. Ann. § 95.011 et seq.	5	4	4	4
Georgia	Ga. Code Ann. § 9-3-20 et seq.	6	4	2	4
Hawaii	Haw. Rev. Stat. § 657-1 et seq.	6	6	2	2
Idaho	Idaho Code § 5-201 et seq.	5	4	2	3
Illinois	735 Ill. Comp. Stat. 5/13-201 et seq.	10	5	2	5

State	Statute	Written Contract	Oral Contract	Injury	Property Damage
Indiana	Ind. Code Ann. § 34-11-2-1 et seq.	10	6	2	6 (real property); 2 (personal property)
Iowa	Iowa Code Ann. § 614.1 et seq.	10	5	2	5
Kansas	Kan. Stat. Ann. § 60-501 et seq.	5	3	2	2
Kentucky	Ky. Rev. Stat. Ann. § 413.080 et seq.	15	5	1	5 (real property); 2 (personal property)
Louisiana	La. civil code § 3492 et seq.	10	10	1	1
Maine	Me. Rev. Stat. Ann. tit. 14, § 751 et seq.	6	6	6	6
Maryland	Md. Courts & Jud. Proc. Code Ann. § 5-101 et seq.	3	3	3	3
Massachusetts	Mass. Ann. Laws ch. 260, § 1 et seq.	6	6	3	3
Michigan	Mich. Comp. Laws § 600.5801 et seq.	6	6	3	3
Minnesota	Minn. Stat. Ann. § 541.01 et seq.	6	6	2	6
Mississippi	Miss. Code. Ann. § 15-1-1 et seq.	6	3	3	3
Missouri	Mo. Rev. Stat. § 516.097 et seq.	5	5	5	5
Montana	Mont. Code Ann. § 27-2-2021 et seq.	8	5	3	2
Nebraska	Neb. Rev. Stat. § 25-201 et seq.	5	4	4	4
Nevada	Nev. Rev. Stat. Ann. § 11.010 et seq.	6	4	2	3
New Hampshire	N.H. Rev. Stat. Ann. § 508:1 et seq.	3	3	3	3
New Jersey	N.J. Stat. Ann. § 2a:14-1 et seq.	6	6	2	6
New Mexico	N.M. Stat. Ann. § 37-1-1 et seq.	6	4	3	4
New York	N.Y. Civ. Prac. Laws & Rules § 201 et seq.	6	6	3	3
North Carolina	N.C. Gen. Stat. § 1-46 et seq.	3	3	3	3
North Dakota	N.D. Cent. Code § 28-01-01 et seq.	6	6	6	6
Ohio	Ohio Rev. Code Ann. § 2305.03 et seq.	8	6	2	4

State	Statute	Written Contract	Oral Contract	Injury	Property Damage
Oklahoma	Okla. Stat. Ann. tit. 12, § 91 et seq.	5	3	2	2
Oregon	Or. Rev. Stat. § 12.010 et seq.	6	6	2	6
Pennsylvania	42 Pa. Cons. Stat. Ann. § 5501 et seq.	4	4	2	2
Rhode Island	R. I. Gen. Laws § 9-1-12 et seq.	10	10	3	10
South Carolina	S.C. Code Ann. § 15-3-510 et seq.	3	3	3	3
South Dakota	S.D. Codified Laws Ann. § 15-2-1 et seq.	6	6	3	6
Tennessee	Tenn. Code Ann. § 28-3-101 et seq.	6	6	1	3
Texas	Tex. Civ. Prac. & Rem. Code § 16.001 et seq.	4	4	2	2
Utah	Utah Code Ann. § 78B-2-101 et seq.	6	4	4	3
Vermont	Vt. Stat. Ann. tit. 12, § 461 et seq.	6	6	3	3
Virginia	Va. Code Ann. § 8.01-228 et seq.	5	3	2	5
Washington	Wash. Rev. Code Ann. § 4.16.005 et seq.	6	3	3	3
West Virginia	W. Va. Code § 55-2-1 et seq.	10	5	2	2
Wisconsin	Wis. Stat. Ann. § 893.01 et seq.	6	6	3	6
Wyoming	Wyo. Stat. § 1-3-102 et seq.	10	8	4	4

Source: Nolo.com.

That's not the end of the complexities and vagaries. What if you incurred the debt in one state but now live in another? Typically, the creditor or collector can choose to use the state with the longer statute.

Also, you can restart an expired statute of limitations in some states by making a payment on an old debt, or just by acknowledging that you owe the money.

Now, you don't have to worry about any of this if the item you're trying to get deleted is a paid collection and is listed that way on your credit report. If it's an unpaid collection, or any unpaid account for that matter, you'll want to do some legal research to make sure that you understand the statutes that apply in your situation:

- If a debt is still within the statute of limitations and it's actually your debt, you want to be careful about disputing the information with the credit bureaus. Remember the phrase, "Let sleeping dogs lie?" You could reawaken interest in collecting the debt by drawing it to the creditor's attention. If you're not prepared to pay the debt or get sued and suffer the potential ding to your credit score that either action could evoke, the better course might be to leave the debt alone and hope it slides silently off your credit report in a few years. (See the next section "Should You Pay Old Debts?" for more details.)

- If the statute of limitations is well past, you can be more aggressive in trying to get an old debt off your report. If you choose this course, though, make sure you don't do anything that could start the statute of limitations all over again.

If you're unwilling to handle all this yourself—and it is a lot to expect a layperson to do—a few good law firms handle cases like this. Use the National Association of Consumer Advocates to get a referral, though, and steer clear of any law firm or other outfit that guarantees results or demands enormous fees in advance.

Should You Pay Old Debts?

Legally, you owe a debt until it's paid, settled, or wiped out in bankruptcy.

Some people erroneously believe that their obligation ends when a creditor charges off the debt. But a charge-off is essentially just an accounting term. The creditor can continue trying to collect or sell the debt to a collection agency, which can try to get you to pay.

Your obligation to pay doesn't end when an unpaid debt falls off your credit report after seven years. The creditor might not be allowed to report the account, but collection actions can continue.

Similarly, your state's statutes of limitations define how long a creditor or collection agency can take you to court over a debt. But even if you can't be sued, a creditor or collector can still ask you to pay.

Given all that, shouldn't you just pay what you owe if you possibly can?

Many people would say yes, pointing out that we have a moral obligation to pay the debts we incur. But the answer to this question is actually trickier than it might appear, for several reasons.

Paying Old Debts Might or Might Not Hurt Your Credit Score

For years, a quirk in the credit-reporting process meant that paying old debts could actually hurt your credit. When the creditor or collection agency updated your credit report to reflect the payment, the FICO formula was often fooled into thinking the old, troubled account was newer than it actually was. Because the formula is designed to weigh recent behavior—good and bad—more heavily than past behavior, anything that looked like you had incurred recent problems could really hurt.

Fair Isaac worked with the credit bureaus to fix this problem. The issue can still pop up, though, if your lender is using an old version of the FICO formula to compute scores. Fair Isaac spokesman Craig Watts said the company doesn't know how many lenders use the old versions, but he thinks it's a "very small percentage" of the total. Still, it's possible that paying old debts could hurt you in the eyes of some creditors.

Just Contacting an Old Creditor Can Leave You Vulnerable to a Lawsuit

Each state has different guidelines on how long a creditor can sue you over a debt, but some states have provisions that allow this statute of limitations to be extended if you make a payment on an old debt or even acknowledge that you owe it. You could be making a good-faith effort to pay your bill or be talked into making a "token" payment as part of negotiations with a collection agency, and the creditor could use that as an excuse to haul you into court and get a judgment against you—an action that might not have been permitted if you had just left the debt unacknowledged and unpaid. The judgment would be a new and serious black mark on your file that could be reported for another seven years.

You're Often Not Dealing with the Original Creditor

The company that you owe the money to might have long since cleared the debt off its books, taken a tax write-off for the loss, and sold the debt—usually for pennies on the dollar—to a collection agency. The original creditor might not accept money if you tried to offer it but would instead direct you to the collector. Many people understandably feel less obligated to a collection agency that bought their debts for a tiny fraction of face value than they do to the company that originally extended the credit.

You Might Be Exposing Yourself to Some Pretty Nasty Characters

Despite laws designed to curb them, some collection agencies employ people who lie to, harass, and abuse borrowers. They might scream at you, use obscene language, or threaten you with jail time. (All these actions are, of course, illegal, but if you don't believe they happen, you need to take a look at my mailbag.)

Even if collectors are polite to your face, they might do things behind your back to further endanger your financial life. Collectors might promise to drop a harmful remark from your credit file and then not follow through—or make the black mark even worse. They might arrange a deal that they say will settle your debt, and then sell the unpaid portion to another agency that renews collection activity. Or they might report any debt you didn't pay to the IRS, which can tax the so-called forgiven debt as income.

More than a few collectors feel that anything they do is justified because—don't you know?—debtors are *bad people*. Collectors have written me insisting that debtors are actually thieves and deserve what they get. The fact that owing money is usually not illegal—but that violating fair credit-reporting and collecting laws is—remains a distinction that completely escapes them.

Problems with collection agencies are so rampant that the FTC typically has more complaints about that industry than any other. The only category that generates more complaints is identity theft. Debt collection accounts for more than one out of ten grievances filed with the agency.

You might still decide to brave all this and try to pay off an old debt. You might feel a strong moral obligation to do so, regardless of the potential consequences. Or you might need to settle a debt because you want to get a mortgage sometime soon. (Lenders typically won't give you a home loan with an open collection on your report.)

If you decide to proceed, make sure you've done your research on the statutes of limitations that apply. (It's tricky, but you can conduct an entire settlement negotiation with a collector without ever acknowledging that you owe the debt—and most attorneys would recommend that's exactly what you should try to do.)

If you can possibly deal with the original creditor, rather than a collection agency, try to do so. Try to get the original creditor to report your account as positively as possible in exchange for your payment. Having the account reported "paid as agreed" would be good. Having the account reported as "settled," however, could leave your score worse off than if you'd left the account open and unpaid. Some credit-repair veterans have had luck getting the creditor to stop reporting the troubled account altogether in exchange for payment, which could be great for your score, although the bureaus strongly discourage this.

If you're dealing with a collection agency, though, push hard to have the entire account deleted. You will have the most leverage if you can make a lump-sum payment, rather than having to make payments. Remember: Any updating that the collection agency does—even if it's to report that you've paid your debt—can make the black mark appear more recent than it is and hurt your score.

If, however, you decide that the cost of paying old bills is greater than the payoff—well, you wouldn't be the first. Some people just decide to donate to their favorite charity an amount equal to the unpaid debt and call it a day.

"But You've Got the Wrong Guy!"

It's not uncommon for debts that you don't owe to pop up on your credit report. Thanks to identity theft, credit bureau mistakes, and greedy collection firms, this happens way too often for comfort.

And you might find yourself truly on the hook for a debt you didn't personally incur.

How can that happen? Here are two of the most common ways:

- **You cosigned a loan for someone else**—If that person doesn't pay, you're legally obligated to foot the bill, and any delinquencies, charge-offs, or collection actions related to the debt will be reported on your credit file. The creditor isn't even required to notify you if the other borrower defaults. The first time you find out about it might well be when it pops up on your credit report.

- **It's a joint account, even if you have since divorced the other account holder**—This one gets people all the time. It doesn't matter what your divorce decree says about who was supposed to pay what. If it's a joint account, it's a joint debt. Your ex can easily trash your report by not paying a joint credit card or mortgage. That's why it's so important to close joint accounts and refinance mortgages and other loans before a divorce is final. I go into more detail in Chapter 12, "Keeping Your Score Healthy."

What if you're just an authorized—rather than a joint—user on someone else's account, and that person's negative information is showing up on your report? If the person added you to the account after opening it and didn't use your income and credit information in the original application, you should dispute the information with the credit bureaus, pointing out that you're not responsible for the debt. You also should ask the original account holder to have your name removed from the account.

If the person used your information and forged your signature to qualify, however, you might need to file a police report to get the creditors to eliminate the information. See Chapter 8, "Identity Theft and Your Credit," for more details.

Part II: Adding Positive Information to Your File

There's more to credit repair than just getting rid of the negative information. You need to ensure that any positive information that can be included in your file actually is.

Try to Get Positive Accounts Reported

You know that the credit bureaus typically don't share information, but it can be frustrating if one of your good, paid-on-time accounts doesn't show up on all your credit reports.

What's worse is when a credit account isn't reported at all. Some creditors simply don't bother to use credit bureau services, and others—usually subprime lenders—deliberately hide the histories of their best customers for fear that their competitors will swoop in.

Although you can't force a creditor to report an account to a bureau or report more frequently, you can always ask.

Sometimes it's all but impossible to get your on-time payments recorded. Most landlords, utility companies, and phone companies will report you to the credit bureaus only if you screw up. (So be sure you don't screw up.)

Borrow Someone Else's History

No, I'm not suggesting that you commit identity theft. Being added to someone else's credit card account as an authorized user can instantly improve your credit report if that person's credit is in good shape. (The opposite can also happen, so make sure you pick the right person.) A cooperative credit issuer exports the card user's account history into your report so that you can benefit from the other person's good financial habits. Not all credit issuers do this export, though, so it's important to call first and ask.

There's another plus to being an authorized, rather than a joint, user: You're not liable for any debt the original account holder runs up.

Get Some Credit or Charge Cards if You Don't Have Any

You need to actively use some plastic to rebuild your score. Although it's anybody's guess how many cards are optimal, it's a safe bet that you'll eventually need more than one.

If you still have accounts you can use, that's great. If your accounts have been closed, you'll need to start from scratch. The plan is outlined in the following sections.

Apply for a Secured Card

Secured cards give you a credit limit that's generally equal to the deposit that you make. You want a card that reports to all three credit bureaus, doesn't charge an application fee or outrageous annual fees, and converts to a regular, unsecured card after 12 months or so of on-time payments. Bankrate. com, CardRatings.com, CreditCards.com, LowCards.com, and NerdWallet, among others, have whole sections on secured cards, including current information about which bank is offering what.

Get Department Store and Gas Cards

These cards tend to be the easiest unsecured plastic you can obtain. After you've had your secured card for a few months, apply for one of these—and perhaps a second one about six months later. Don't rush this process, because applying for too much credit in too short a time period can hurt your score.

Get an Installment Loan

You might take out a small, personal loan from your bank or credit bureau and pay it back over time. Or you might, as our friend Chance did, simply "suck it up" and go for a high-rate auto loan:

"My first vehicle loan out of BK was at 21 percent interest. After paying this for about two years, I traded it in and purchased another," Chance wrote. "The next [loan rate was] at 13.99 percent. [I paid] this for a year [and] then refinanced online for 7.95 percent. Then [I] traded it in, and now I have a 6 percent auto loan."

I can't advise buying three cars in five years like Chance did. But you should try to make sure you're not tying yourself to a long-term loan at usurious rates. Get a shorter loan, if you possibly can, and make a decent down payment to make sure you have some equity in the vehicle so that you can refinance it when your credit improves.

Consider a Cosigner

If you can't get a loan on your own, you can try to find a cosigner to facilitate the deal. But realize that person is putting his credit history on the line for you. If you mess up, your cosigner pays the price because he's just as legally obligated to pay the debt as you are.

Make Sure Your Credit Limits Are Correct

This is a point that many credit rebuilders unfortunately overlook. A big chunk of your credit score has to do with how much of your available credit you're using. If the credit limits are showing up on your report as lower than they actually are, your debt utilization ratio will be higher than it needs to be. You can use the dispute process, but it might be just as expeditious to call your creditors and ask them to update your credit bureau files.

Part III: Use Your Credit Well

You might want to review the information in Chapter 4 on improving your score the right way. When you're rebuilding after a disaster, you need to be particularly careful about what's discussed in this section.

Pay Bills on Time

Remember: The biggest chunk of your credit score is likely to be your payment history, and even one late payment can be devastating. Become religious about making sure all your bills are paid on time, all the time.

If you get an installment loan, set up an automatic payment system— either direct withdrawals from your checking account or automatic, recurring payments through an online bill paying system. Leave nothing to chance.

Use the Credit You Have

Make a few small purchases every month with your plastic—but no more than you can pay off each month. If you worry that you'll give in to temptation if you carry your card with you, arrange to have some small monthly bill, such as an online game subscription or health club dues, charged to the card each month. Then set up an automatic payment from your checking account. That way the card is being used and the bill is being paid without your having to think about it.

Keep Your Balances Low

Somebody who has good credit can occasionally afford to run up a big balance on a credit card. That's not you. It doesn't matter if your credit limits on your new cards are ridiculously low. You never want to use more than about 30 percent of the limits you have; 20 percent or less is better, and 10 percent or less is best. If you go over 30 percent, try to make a payment before the statement closes to reduce the balance that's reported to the credit bureaus.

You can keep track of your purchases in a checkbook register, or just check your balances frequently at the card's Web site. Quicken or Mint personal finance software can also help you monitor your balances.

Remember: These cards are not for your convenience—and they certainly shouldn't be an excuse for you to carry debt. The plastic you have now is meant to help rehabilitate your beaten-up credit.

Pace Yourself

It's never a good idea to apply for a bunch of new credit in a short period of time. That's particularly true when you're trying to rebuild a score. It's not a bad idea to wait at least six months between applications for credit. Don't apply for cards just to see whether you'll be accepted, and do try to target your applications to lenders that are likely to want your business. A recently bankrupted person who applies for a low-rate card from a major issuer is just asking to get turned down—and have another ding added to her file.

Don't Commit the Biggest Credit-Repair Mistakes

You can see from the information in this chapter that fixing your credit can be a long and involved process, with many opportunities for the novice to make a mistake. Three of the biggest mistakes you should avoid are spelled out here.

Hiring a Fly-by-Night Firm

The Federal Trade Commission is constantly trying to stamp out scam artists promising instant credit repair, but like cockroaches, they always return. You can pretty much assume a scam if the company guarantees its results in advance, wants to charge you a big, upfront fee, or suggests you create a "new" credit report by using a different Social Security or taxpayer identification number.

Most people can handle their own credit repair without paying big fees or committing fraud. If you run into problems, look for a legitimate law firm through the National Association of Consumer Advocates at www.naca.net for help.

Failing to Get It All in Writing

The phone is not your friend. Although you can and should take copious notes if you ever have to have a phone conversation with a creditor, collector, or credit bureau, you're much better off conducting credit repair in writing.

Reviving the Statute of Limitations

States have differing rules about how long a creditor can sue you over a debt, with most limiting the period to three to six years. Making a payment on an old debt, or even acknowledging that you owe it, can revive that statute and leave you vulnerable to a lawsuit. Make sure you know the rules for your state when dealing with old debts.

DID CREDIT CARD REFORM HURT BORROWERS?

The CARD Act of 2009 was designed to rein in some of the credit card industry's more egregious practices, such as raising rates retroactively for any reason or no reason, moving due dates and instituting due "times" to increase late fee revenue, and approving over-limit transactions so issuers could slap borrowers with even more fees.

The credit card companies, of course, fought the changes, warning they would raise the costs for using a credit card; that hasn't turned out to be the case. Although some issuers experimented with instituting annual fees, the majority of new card offers, including rewards cards, still come with no annual fee, according to CreditCards.com. Meanwhile, the amount of late fees people pay has dropped by half, and over-limit fees have virtually disappeared, according to a review by the Consumer Financial Protection Bureau.

Interest rates on average have risen, but lenders continue to pump out low-rate and 0 percent offers to those with excellent credit. In any case, it would be hard to know how much of the rate increase was due to the CARD Act and how much was due to the credit crunch, financial crisis, and subsequent recession. Banks that suffered massive losses were under pressure to produce revenue where they could, and raising rates on credit cards was one easy way to do that.

Changes in the availability of credit certainly have more to do with the financial crisis and its fallout than any legislative acts. Starting in late 2007, nervous lenders began reeling in credit lines and raising rates as the credit crunch took hold. As the 2008 financial crisis unfolded, many lenders abandoned the subprime lending market. Just as more people were being forced into bankruptcy by job loss and losing their homes to foreclosure, banks were making it much tougher to get the kinds of cards and loans that could help stricken borrowers rebuild their scores. As the economy improved, though, more lenders became willing to extend credit to less-than-prime customers.

8

Identity Theft and Your Credit

Massive database breaches still make the headlines, but hacks that expose millions of people's sensitive personal information have become distressingly routine.

The Target breach affected as many as 110 million customers whose credit and debit account numbers were stored in the retailer's database. The Anthem breach exposed Social Security numbers and other data of 80 million current and former customers of the health insurer. The federal Office of Personnel Management had to notify more than 20 million people that their information had been compromised. The IRS, which pays out billions in phony tax refunds each year, had to temporarily shut down its transcript service after hackers successfully cleared security questions in 50 percent of their 610,000 attempts—indicating they already had extensive information about the victims; and access to tax returns gave them even more.

These are just some of the most notorious incursions. Breaches at retailers, financial institutions, government agencies, schools, medical providers, law offices, and more are daily occurrences. So far, nearly 1 billion records have been compromised in known database breaches, according to the Privacy Rights Clearinghouse.

Identity theft is such a rapidly growing crime that some experts say it's no longer a matter of *whether* you'll become a victim, it's a matter of *when*. The annual costs of this crime are staggering:

- Billions of dollars in losses to businesses and institutions

- Millions of dollars in out-of-pocket expenses for consumers

- Hundreds of millions of hours spent by consumers trying to resolve the problem, stop the fraud, and clear up their credit reports

Identity theft encompasses a variety of crimes, from stealing someone's credit card number to opening accounts in the victim's name. About 15 percent of victims report that their identities were stolen for purposes other than obtaining credit, such as to get government documents, commit tax fraud, or mislead police. Some people give phony names and Social Security numbers when arrested or stopped for a traffic violation.

The most common type of identity theft is "account takeover," where your existing credit or debit cards are commandeered. More costly is "new account" fraud, where thieves take over your identity wholesale. By pretending to be you, they can open up credit card accounts, get an auto loan, be treated at a hospital, or rent an apartment. When the bills are due, they don't pay—and those delinquencies, charge-offs, collections, repossessions, evictions, and judgments wind up on your credit report, sending your credit score into the basement.

The FTC's estimate of the time that consumers spend clearing up problems—30 hours on average—was decried by many identity theft experts as far too low. The Identity Theft Resource Center said that many victims spend 300 to 600 hours dealing with the various problems that identity thieves cause.

Often, the biggest time-consumer is trying to get fraudulent accounts expunged from credit reports. Many victims complain they get the runaround from credit bureaus. The bureaus say the problem is lenders, who continue to report account information to the bureaus even after they've been told the accounts might be fraudulent. Either way, the ID theft victim gets squeezed.

Michel, a successful businessman in Sherman Oaks, California, spent months trying to convince the three credit bureaus to remove delinquent accounts from his credit report before finally hiring a lawyer:

"It took me almost a year and thousands of dollars to finally clean up my report. In the meantime, I lost out on the lowest mortgage rates in years as a result," Michel said. "The whole system is totally unfair as the three majors believe the creditors and make it virtually impossible to remove an item unless you hire an attorney."

Michel might overstate the case, but he does reflect the frustration experienced by many identity theft victims trying to clear their names, said Linda Foley, former codirector of the Identity Theft Resource Center and an ID theft victim herself.

Even if you're successful in getting your reports cleaned up, your work might not be done. After identity thieves find someone who has good credit, they can strike over and over again. Mary in Charlotte, North Carolina, has been hit four times so far:

"I do everything the experts say," Mary said. "I have a shredder... I don't even mail bills from my home."

Although three of the incidents involved existing accounts, the fourth involved new credit cards:

"The criminal racked up thousands in credit card debt under my name... and had the bills mailed somewhere else," Mary said.

Mary was clueless about the debt until she tried to apply for a cell phone and was turned down.

Here are just a few of the ways your identity can be stolen:

- You hand your credit card to a waiter in a restaurant. Out of your sight, the waiter runs the card through a small, handheld device called a skimmer. All the relevant information contained on your card's black magnetic strip—including your name and the account number—is stored in the device and can be used to create new cards.

- You fill out an application for credit, an apartment, insurance, or employment. A crooked employee sells the information to a ring of identity thieves or uses it herself to open accounts. Or perhaps the employees are honest, but the business tosses the application into the trash, where any dumpster diver could find it.

- Hackers break into online databases where your personal financial data is stored. Such breaches are now being made public, thanks to state laws that require residents to be notified when their private details have been compromised.

- Stolen laptops and lost backup computer tapes are another common way that sensitive information falls into the wrong hands.

- Dishonest employees or thieves pretending to be legitimate businesses gain access to records that they can use for identity theft.

You might notice a common thread to these examples: There's precious little you, as an individual, could have done to prevent these crimes.

Sure, you could stop using plastic at restaurants, refuse to fill out any more applications, and cancel all your credit cards, but there's still enough information about you floating around out there for a thief to use.

This is a point missed in most identity theft articles, which tend to focus on simplistic solutions such as "Buy a shredder!" and "Get a locking mailbox!" Yes, these measures can help, and later in this chapter you'll find quite a few more preventive suggestions. But they don't change the fact that much of your exposure to identity theft is beyond your control.

If you really want to see why identity theft is epidemic, look no further than your own wallet. Chances are if you have one credit card, you have five, and just about every chain store you walk into is trying to get you to apply for another. Lenders offer instant credit, send out billions of preapproved applications, and mail customers so-called convenience checks that thieves can fish out of the mail or trash.

You've probably heard the stories about dogs being sent credit card applications; Diane of Santa Barbara got one for her two-year-old:

"I could not and still cannot believe that credit card companies are not held more responsible for giving out credit," Diane said, "without truly checking the background of the individuals to whom they provide credit."

Even without a prefilled form, identity thieves have discovered that getting approved for new credit is quite easy. Lenders may not require photo IDs, and some accept incorrect addresses and misspelled names. Often, all the thief needs is your Social Security number and an approximate spelling of your name.

Tom Richards of Huntington Beach, California, said a thief convinced Sears by phone to issue two MasterCards in Richards's name—and then send them to an address not listed on Richards's credit report.

The application was fishy enough that Sears sent a letter to Richards's actual address, informing him that the cards had been issued. That allowed Richards to report the fraud. But it made him wonder why Sears would open the account in the first place.

Simply put, the answer is money. The more credit that lenders and retailers can extend, the more money they can make. Speed is key, and most lenders' computerized processes are designed to make decisions in seconds. If the decisions are wrong, most lenders can easily absorb the costs of the resulting fraud. The costs that consumers pay—in out-of-pocket expenses, time, and legal fees trying to clear up their credit reports—aren't taken into account.

Incredibly enough, some lenders are in such a hurry that they even ignore fraud alerts, which are the flags that identity theft victims can put on their credit reports to let lenders know their credit has been misused and to indicate that they want to be contacted personally if credit applications are submitted in their names. Some lenders feel the extra step is too expensive, whereas others never see the alert because they buy truncated credit information that doesn't include the red flag.

Options That Might Help

As the cost of identity theft rises, a few tools have been created to help you fight back.

Credit Freezes

The growing problem of identity theft prompted California to pioneer an innovative solution: Allow people to shut off or "freeze" their credit reports so that no one can open new accounts in their names. People who opt for a credit freeze are issued a personal identification number that they can use to "unfreeze" their reports when they want to apply for credit.

The solution was so simple and effective that other states adopted similar laws. After more than half of the states passed legislation, the three credit unions capitulated and offered credit freezes to anyone who wanted one. You'll find more details later in this chapter.

FACTA Rights

There also have been some federal law changes that may help identity theft victims get back some control of their lives. Most of these changes were contained in the Fair and Accurate Credit Transactions Act (FACTA). According to a summation by Consumers Union, the law includes the following provisions:

- If a fraud alert is on a consumer's credit report, lenders are required to phone the consumer or take other "reasonable steps" to verify the applicant's identity before issuing credit or raising a credit limit. The alert must be included with any credit report or score sold to lenders.

- When a consumer files a fraud alert with one bureau, that bureau is required to contact the others so that alerts can be put on their records as well.

- Credit bureaus are required to stop reporting accounts or account information that a consumer identifies as fraudulent if the consumer provides an identity theft report filed with a police agency. This procedure is known as *trade line blocking*.

- After a bureau informs a creditor that a block is in effect, the creditor must have "reasonable" procedures to keep it from reporting the bad information again and "repolluting" the consumer's file.

- When a block is in effect, creditors are prohibited from selling or transferring the debt to a collection agency. If the debt is already in collections, the collector is required to notify the original creditor that the debt might be fraudulent and to notify the consumer of his collection rights—if the consumer asks for such a notice.

- Businesses where a thief has opened accounts have new duties to produce records that the ID theft victim might need to clear his name. The businesses, however, can require the ID theft victim to get an actual police report (which is different, and more difficult to get, than an affidavit filed with a police agency).

- Merchants are required to truncate all credit and debit card numbers on receipts, and consumers can request that the credit reports sent to them show truncated Social Security numbers.

Identity theft experts worry that Congress gave lenders several big loopholes, such as allowing them to take "reasonable steps" for identity verification rather than requiring phone contact. They note that many law enforcement agencies still refuse to take identity theft seriously and won't create police reports or accept affidavits. They point out that creditors and credit bureaus are already prohibited from reporting false information by the Fair Credit Reporting Act. In any case, you still need to be vigilant about monitoring and protecting your credit.

Chip-and-PIN Cards

It took the huge Target security breach, which compromised people's credit and debit card numbers, to finally push U.S. retailers and bankers toward the superior chip-and-PIN technology used by most of the rest of the world. In 2015, retailers began installing new point-of-sale terminals, and banks began issuing cards embedded with hard-to-counterfeit computer chips that issue unique, one-time transaction codes to verify purchases.

Those codes are pretty much useless to hackers, so when chip-and-PIN use is standard, retailers' databases will be less attractive.

How to Reduce Your Exposure to Identity Theft

You can do several things to reduce the possibility of having your identity stolen.

Buy a Shredder

You can get a shredder for less than $20 at an office supply store, and no home should be without one. Even better would be to spend $100 or so and get a cross-cut shredder, which chops paper and other media into tiny pieces. Anything that includes personal financial information or your Social Security number should be shredded before it's sent to the trash.

Get a Locking Mailbox

Think of all the bounty that comes into your mailbox—bank statements, credit cards, credit card offers, "convenience checks" you can write against your accounts, health insurance documents with your Social Security numbers printed on them...the list goes on and on. Some identity thieves simply follow the postal carrier around and snatch what they want from unprotected mailboxes.

Protect Your Outgoing Mail

Think of all that goes out in your mail, including checks and credit card account numbers on the coupons you use to pay your bills. If you still rely on snail mail to pay your bills, use the post office nearest to you to send all your mail, rather than leaving it out where anyone can get it. Better yet, consider signing up for online bill payment, which offers encryption and other security measures to keep your transactions safe from criminals. (Hacking incidents typically target big unencrypted databases sitting in poorly guarded mainframe computers, not the heavily protected transactions that zip back and forth between consumers and their banks or merchants.)

Be Careful with Your Tax Returns

Sending tax returns and tax payments through the mail is inherently insecure because a thief or dishonest postal employee can intercept the envelope. Filing by mail also delays the processing of your return and any refund you're owed because the IRS has to convert your information into an electronic format. File your tax returns electronically instead for a more secure transmission. The IRS has free systems to electronically pay any tax you owe: individuals can use the Direct Pay service, and businesses can use the Electronic Federal Tax Payment System.

Also, file as early as possible to reduce the chances of refund theft.

Keep Your Financial Documents Under Lock and Key

How easy would it be for a repairman to walk off with your checkbook, or for a guest in your home to rifle through your files? Most people are perfectly trustworthy, but enough aren't that you should take steps to secure your checks and files.

Get Stingy with Your Social Security Number

This nine-digit number was never meant to be an all-purpose identifier, but that's exactly how many businesses use it. Everyone from your dry cleaner to your vet might ask for it, but few have the right to demand it.

You need to give your Social Security number to employers, financial institutions, and certain government agencies, such as your state's Department of Motor Vehicles. Your Social Security number is also important for credit transactions. Many insurers use the number as an identifier, or to run credit checks to determine your premiums (see Chapter 10, "Insurance and Your Credit Score").

Beyond that, however, try to keep your number to yourself. If the business insists that it needs the number, you can either do business with someone else or "misremember" a digit or nine to protect your privacy.

Know What's in Your Wallet

Obviously, you shouldn't carry your Social Security number with you or have it printed on your checks. You should also lobby your health insurer to print "Participant's SSN" rather than the actual number on your card. This system is working fine in California, which led the nation in privacy protections by insisting that health insurers stop printing the numbers on health cards by 2005. Many did so well before the deadline.

Beyond that, try to carry as few credit and debit cards as possible. The more you carry, the more chances that an identity thief has to wreck your credit if your wallet is stolen.

If you have your wallet stolen, don't wait until you get home to report stolen credit cards. Program your cell to include emergency numbers for the major issuers, and call them to report the theft: 1-800-Visa 911, 1-800-MasterCard, 1-800-Discover, and 1-800-528-4800 for American Express. These are among the most valuable cards to thieves and should be shut down right away. When you get home (or back to your hotel, if you're traveling), you can work on canceling the rest.

It can help to periodically empty your wallet onto a photocopier and get an image of both sides of every card, plus your driver's license. This will make it easier for you to report the thefts and get replacement cards. (Just remember to put the cards back in your wallet and keep copies in a safe place. You don't want to leave your financial life lying around at the local Kinko's.)

Ask About Shredding Policies

If you're required to give personal financial information to any business or professional, ask how they dispose of old documents. If the business doesn't have a secure disposal policy in place, take your business elsewhere or press it to institute one. Federal law requires businesses to discard records with consumer information in a way that prevents unauthorized access.

The law gives businesses some leeway about what methods to use, but you can always make specific requests. It's not too much to ask, for example, that your accountant shred copies of your old tax returns, or at least call you so that you can come pick them up and do the same. Ditto for your doctor or any other professional.

Don't Let Your Debit Card out of Your Sight

If your ATM card has a Visa or MasterCard logo, it's known as a debit or check card and can be used just like a credit card, without punching in a personal identification number. A thief who swipes it or skims the information off the magnetic stripe can quickly empty your bank account.

The good news is that banks won't hold you responsible for fraud committed with a debit card with a Visa or MasterCard logo, but you can still wind up without money for a few days before the bank restores the stolen cash. That's why it's better to use a credit card or cash anywhere you won't be able to monitor the actual transaction (such as when you hand payment to a waiter in a restaurant).

Mary, the four-time identity theft victim, also refuses to use her debit card at fast food restaurants, gas stations, or mom-and-pop type stores:

"These small business do not do background checks on employees, they typically have high turnover rates, and [they] are prime targets for transient-type workers," Mary said. "Any criminal [who] engages in identity theft for a living knows they can wait tables for a month and get tons of card numbers to use or sell."

You should be particularly careful about gas stations, many of which have resisted efforts to upgrade their pumps to encrypt PINs. That's right—a gas pump may be storing your PIN in easy-to-read form, just waiting for a thief to access it.

This should be obvious, but don't give your credit or debit cards to anyone else to use. A small but significant portion of fraud and identity theft is committed by family members, friends, and lovers—either current or ex.

Some of the most heartbreaking cases are when a parent snatches the identity of a child (see "When Parents Steal," later in this chapter).

Monitor Your Accounts

A quick glance at your monthly statement is no longer enough. Criminals often test stolen cards by making a small transaction or two before cleaning you out. Other bad guys simply make relatively small regular charges on thousands of accounts, scoring millions of dollars because of their victims' inattention.

You should be checking your bank and credit accounts at least weekly, if not daily. Make sure your institutions have up-to-date contact information—both email and cell—so that they can warn you of possible fraudulent actions, including attempts to change your address. Set up account alerts so that you're made aware of "card not present" and foreign transactions.

Ideally, your institution offers "two-factor authentication," which requires something you know—such as a password—and something you have—such as a code texted to your cell. Many banks don't offer this technology, unfortunately, even though it's a much better way to protect your accounts against incursions than using security questions. Ask your institution if two-factor authentication is available, and use it if it is. Otherwise, perhaps you should consider switching to an institution that cares a little more about account security.

Opt Out of Credit Card Solicitations, Junk Mail, and Telemarketing

The credit bureaus have a toll-free number (888-5OPT-OUT) that allows you to take your name off marketing lists that are sold to credit card companies. Signing up won't eliminate credit card solicitations, but it will cut down the volume significantly. The fewer such offers in the mail, the fewer chances that thieves will have to steal them.

You can contact the Direct Marketing Association to be removed from its mail and phone lists, as well. Go to www.dmachoice.org or write to DMA Choice, Direct Marketing Association, P.O. Box 643, Carmel, NY 10512. Also register for the federal Do Not Call registry at www.donotcall.gov or 1-888-382-1222. If a solicitor calls you after you've been on the registry at least three months—and the caller isn't a charity, survey taker, political fundraiser, or a company that you already do business with—odds are good it's a scam artist because a legitimate company would abide by the do-not-call list.

Unfortunately, calls violating the Do Not Call registry have exploded in recent years. To fight back, the Federal Communications Commission in 2015 okayed call-blocking technology and denied requests from bankers, telemarketers, and bill collectors that could have increased junk calls to cell phones.

Be Cautious About Using Your Smartphone for Financial Matters

Cell (and cordless) phones are much more secure than they used to be. Years ago, readily available radio scanners allowed others to easily listen in on analog signals emitted by many cheap cordless phones and by some cell phones that have the capability to switch from digital to analog signals. Today's cordless phones use digital spread-spectrum technology, scramble the signal, and operate on higher frequencies, while cell phone users typically have more secure technology as well.

As cell phones have evolved into smartphones, though, we've potentially given the bad guys a whole bunch of new ways to steal our information and invade our privacy. Smartphones can make banking and other financial tasks more convenient, but we need to be wary of bogus Wi-Fi networks or the possibility of our phones being stolen. It's important to

- Use a password or passcode on your phone

- Install a "find my phone" app that allows remote erasure of data

- Don't allow your phone to automatically connect to available Wi-Fi networks or Bluetooth connections

Also refrain from discussing any sensitive matters on your cell, especially if you can be overheard. You've always been more at risk because of your own booming voice than from any scanner-equipped eavesdropper.

Be Wary of Telephone Solicitors and Emails Purporting to Be from Financial Institutions

Don't give out your credit card number, Social Security number, or other sensitive financial information by email, and don't do it by phone unless you initiated the contact. Even then, make sure that you trust the business before divulging any information.

Criminals have become increasingly proficient at *phishing*, a fraud that typically uses an email purporting to be from your bank or credit card issuer and that directs you to a look-alike Web site where you're supposed to input your account numbers. If a financial institution contacts you, call them using the toll-free number on your statement or the back of your credit or debit card rather than a number or link provided on an email or Web site.

Be Smarter About Social Media

"I can't believe you did this!" your friend posts on your Facebook wall, along with a link to what looks like a racy video. You click on the link, only to land on what looks like another Facebook page asking for your ID and password. Thinking you've hit a glitch, you enter them again—except the second page was a decoy, and the original post was from a hacker who used similar tactics to break into your friend's account, and who will use yours to lure other victims. You've just given the bad guys entrée into your personal and perhaps financial world, as well as that of your friends. The ID and password the evil-doers collect may be used to hack your financial or other accounts, if you use the same set for different sites, plus you probably have enough private information posted on your account for the hacker to figure out other passwords you might use (such as those containing the name of your child or your pet).

You don't have to abandon social media to protect your identity, but you do need to be careful about how you use it. For example:

- **Set your privacy settings high**—Social media sites seem to be constantly thinking up ways to invade your privacy, so you'll want to keep up to date on their latest "innovations" and how to thwart them, if necessary. The site Lifehacker typically has excellent tutorials on how to make your social media accounts more secure and private.

- **Don't post information that could help hackers**—Financial institutions and other sites include challenge questions to try to verify you're really you when you, for example, lose your password and need to reset it. This information can include, but is not limited to, details such as your birthdate, your mother's maiden name, the name of your first pet, where you went to elementary school, and so on. Security questions are a pretty lousy way to protect your accounts, as the IRS transcript hack proved; but as long as sites insist on using them, you should opt for hard-to-guess answers.

- **Practice good password hygiene**—Create strong passwords,
  use different ones for different sites, and change them often.
  Strong passwords include letters, numbers, and symbols; are
  at least eight characters long (ten is better); and aren't easy
  to guess. One way to create a strong password is to think of a
  phrase, such as "Into the breach once more," using the first and
  third letters of each word: ittebeocmr. Capitalize the second
  or third letter and replace letters with look-alike numbers or
  symbols: iTt3b30@mr. Most browsers will store these passwords for you, allowing for easy retrieval, although there is
  some risk your browser could be hacked; another solution is
  to use a password storage site or program such as LastPass or
  1Password, which uses state-of-the-art encryption. If you can't
  be troubled to do anything else, at least use different passwords
  on social media than you do on your financial sites.

Safeguard Your Social Security Number

Until 2011, the Social Security Administration (SSA) sent out statements to
every worker that summarized their earnings and estimated the benefits they,
and their families, could expect. The statements were a great tool to make
sure you were being properly credited for all the taxes you've paid into the
system. But the statements also helped people spot fraud. Missing earnings
or earnings that aren't yours can be a tip-off that someone else was using
your number.

The SSA ended the wholesale mailings as a money-saving measure but
under pressure restored them to people 60 and over in 2012. Two years later,
the administration started mailing paper statements at five-year intervals to
workers 25 and older who hadn't established online accounts at www.ssa.
gov/my account.

By federal law, you typically have only three years to correct earnings
reporting errors, so you may want to check the records for your last few years
of earnings every three years.

Monitor Your Credit Reports

A few years ago, it was enough to check your credit report annually. Now,
many identity theft experts recommend that you review your reports at least
twice a year, if not more often. The first hint you might have that you're a
victim is often a suspicious entry on your credit report.

Should you spring for one of those credit-monitoring services that promise to do the work for you? Maybe not. Read on.

Does Credit Monitoring Work?

The public's rising concern about identity theft has prompted the credit bureaus and other companies to see a lucrative marketing opportunity. The result is credit monitoring, or services that promise to watch over your credit report and alert you if anything suspicious occurs.

Credit-monitoring and similar "privacy-protection" services are now a multibillion-dollar industry. What credit monitoring can't do is *prevent* identity theft, despite marketers' claims that it provides "protection" against such crimes. Credit-monitoring services can't snatch credit applications out of thieves' hands or prevent lenders from opening accounts for the wrong people. What the better services can do is give you some early warning that there's a problem, which can give you a head start in cleaning up the mess.

The quality, however, varies widely, and most credit-monitoring services have serious drawbacks:

- **They're not all comprehensive**—The better services promise to check your report at all three credit bureaus, but some provide ongoing monitoring of your report at only one bureau, with only periodic checks of the other two. These periodic checks usually happen once every three months, but they might be annual. Some services stick solely to one bureau and never check in at the other two.

- **They might not provide much of a head start**—The best services promise to alert you within 24 hours if someone applies for credit in your name. Others settle for weekly, monthly, or even quarterly updates. Again, because most don't provide daily monitoring of all three bureaus, ID theft might not be detected for months.

- **They're costly**—Although some services cost as little as $5 a month, most will set you back $10 to $15—or more. Over time, those fees can add up and may not be a good value, particularly if you're not at high risk of becoming a victim.

Many ID theft experts suggest that most people are better off requesting their reports periodically from the bureaus, rather than paying for credit monitoring. Consider rotating your requests, so that you first get a report from Experian, then three months later one from TransUnion, and then three months after that one from Equifax. If you keep up the rotation, you'll see each bureau's report at least twice every 12 months for much less than you'd pay a credit-monitoring service.

If you do decide you want a monitoring service's help, though, make sure you find out the following:

- How often your report is checked at each bureau, and how often those reports are updated.

- How quickly you'll be sent an email if something suspicious occurs. Find out the longest that a problem could appear on your report at any of the bureaus before the service would bring it to your attention.

- How much the service costs and how often you will be charged.

- What other services are provided (identity theft insurance, concierge help in reporting identity theft) and how you can access those services.

Consider a Credit Freeze

For many consumers, a credit freeze is overkill. The freezes typically involve setup fees of $10 to $15 per credit bureau, plus similar fees if you want to temporarily lift the freeze to get credit. You might find it inconvenient to be cut off from those "instant credit" deals that offer discounts when you sign up for an account. But others, including the following, will find a credit freeze to be a great solution:

- Victims of "new account" fraud. Some kinds of identity theft are relatively easy to deal with, such as when your credit card number is fraudulently used. In that case, you're issued a new card, and the chances of your being victimized again are hardly greater than that of the rest of the population. If someone's tried to open accounts in your name, though, they probably know enough about you to try again.

- People who have been informed that their personal identifying information—their name, address, Social Security number, date of birth—has been compromised by a database breach or other incident.

- Those whose wallets are missing. A stolen purse or wallet can be a gold mine for an identity thief, especially if your Social Security number were inside.

- Relatives, friends, or acquaintances of a thief or potential thief. If a family member has stolen one relative's identity, he might steal another's. Likewise, be cautious of addicts, gamblers, and others feeding compulsions because they might view your credit as an easy route to more money to feed their addictions. In fact, anyone who has a compromised moral sense and access to your personal information could be a potential thief, so keep your data as protected as possible even in your own home.

- Anyone who can't sleep at night without a freeze. If your state allows you to freeze your credit and you'd feel better with your reports locked up, then by all means, do so.

Each of the three credit bureaus has information on its site about how to institute a freeze.

What to Do if You're Already a Victim

The only good news about the rise in identity theft is that there are now more resources than ever before to help victims. You still need to gird yourself for battle with credit bureaus, creditors, and even collection agencies, but you're not out there alone.

The Federal Trade Commission has extensive information for ID theft victims at www.consumer.gov/idtheft, or you can call 1-877-FTC-HELP (1-877-382-4357) to get free information. You also can find helpful resources at the Identity Theft Resource Center (www.idtheftcenter.org or 1-858-693-7935) and the Privacy Rights Clearinghouse (www.privacyrights.org or 1-619-298-3396), among other locations.

Some financial institutions are remarkably responsive to identity theft victims, whereas others presume that anyone reporting ID theft is a liar until proven otherwise. Either way, you'll want to be assertive, persistent, and relentless in your efforts to clear your name. The Privacy Rights Clearinghouse, the California Public Interest Research Group, and the Identity Theft Resource Center suggest that you take the steps outlined in the next sections.

Keep Good Notes of Every Conversation You Have Regarding the ID Theft

Include dates, times, and first and last names, if possible, of everyone you contact. (It can be helpful to use one notebook in which you jot everything down so that your notes aren't scattered all over the house.) Follow up these conversations in writing, with letters sent certified mail, return receipt requested. Keep track of the hours and costs you're incurring; you might be eligible for restitution if the thief is caught and prosecuted.

Contact the Credit Bureaus by Phone and Then with a Follow-Up in Writing

At the very least, add a fraud alert to your credit file and to make sure the alert is for seven years, rather than any shorter period. (When you're not a victim, you can get fraud alerts only for 90 days at a time.) Fraud alerts can make "instant" credit more difficult to obtain, but you can always cancel an alert later if you want.

The bureaus have a system that is supposed to allow you to alert all three companies with a single call. There have been some questions, though, about whether the bureaus are properly sharing this information. So after you set up a fraud alert, make sure the fraud notation has been added.

The credit bureaus should supply you with contact information for any creditors listed on your credit report. You can set up a fraud alert with one of the bureaus online, or you can call Equifax at 1-800-525-6285, Experian at 1-888-397-3742, or TransUnion at 1-800-680-7289.

If the theft involved opening new accounts, you should also consider a credit freeze.

Contact the Creditors by Phone and Then Follow Up in Writing

If someone is using one of your existing credit or bank accounts to run up charges, the bank or lender typically closes the account and issues you a new one, along with some kind of form or affidavit to report the fraud. If new accounts have been opened, the financial institution also asks you to fill out a fraud affidavit. Many accept the uniform fraud affidavit available on the FTC Web site.

Contact the Police or Local Sheriff

Some jurisdictions are terrific about taking identity theft reports, and some aren't—even though it's a federal crime (18 USC 1028) to assume someone else's identity. Be persistent, bring as much documentation of the fraud as you can, and try to get the law enforcement agency to list the affected accounts on the report. A police report can help enormously in getting problems resolved with creditors.

Contact Bank and Checking Verification Companies

If the thief set up phony bank accounts in your name or stole checks, you need to close those accounts and stop payment on any outstanding checks. Open new checking and savings accounts and contact the major check-verification companies to report the theft. Here are some of those companies:

- **ChexSystems**—1-800-428-9623 or www.chexhelp.com

- **TeleCheck**—1-800-710-9898 or www.telecheck.com

Contact the Collection Agencies

FACTA legislation made it illegal for fraudulent accounts to be turned over to collections, but that doesn't mean it won't happen—or doesn't help you much if it's happened already.

Dealing with collection agencies can be especially difficult because they're used to dealing with bad debts every day and have heard every excuse in the book—including many false claims of identity theft. In addition, more than a few collectors are unresponsive, unethical, and abusive in their dealings with consumers. Tread carefully here, but don't give up. The Identity Theft Resource Center has a separate fact sheet (FS 116) on how to cope. The following are some of the suggestions:

- In addition to keeping good notes and following up in writing (certified mail, return receipt requested), ask for a written statement from the collector outlining any agreements or decisions you discuss. Ask for confirmation in writing that you don't owe the debt and that the account has been closed.

- Stay cool and calm. The more professional you act, the more likely the collection agency will treat you seriously.

- Ask for a supervisor or the company's fraud investigator. Customer service representatives are usually little help.

- Tell the collector that you are a victim of identity theft and you are not responsible for the account. Don't say that you "dispute" the account because collection agencies associate that word with people who are arguing about the amounts they owe or trying to evade a legitimate debt.

Collection protocols for dealing with identity theft are constantly evolving, so contact the center for more details on your rights and the best approaches.

Get Legal Help

If your efforts to solve the problem yourself aren't working, you might need to hire a lawyer. You can get referrals from your local bar association, legal aid office, or the National Association of Consumer Advocates at www.naca. net.

Don't Give Up

Be determined to be the last one standing when this is over. Don't pay bills that aren't yours to get a creditor off your back and don't file for bankruptcy. If a creditor or collector threatens you with a lawsuit, jail time, or other punishment, point out calmly that such threats are violations of federal debt-collecting and credit-reporting laws. Then report them to the Federal Trade Commission and your state attorney general's office.

When Parents Steal

Michelle was a Kentucky college student when she discovered an awful fact: Her credit score had been trashed by her mother, who had taken out more than ten credit cards in Michelle's name and failed to pay debts totaling more than $12,000:

> *"No one would believe me, not police, judges, lawyers,"*
> *Michelle said. "I was harassed by collectors telling*
> *me I was a liar."*

Michelle has since found a lawyer who's trying, for free, to help her clear her name. But it's an uphill battle. Although several of the accounts were opened when Michelle was under 18—a minor and obviously too young to be held to a contract—many of the credit card companies are refusing to drop the black marks from her credit report:

> *"I have spent so much time in tears, worry, depression, and rage over this ordeal," Michelle said. "I can't get a new credit card, and when I moved off campus last year, my roommate had to sign the lease because my credit was too bad to get an apartment."*

What's worse, Michelle said, is her mother's reaction to the chaos she created in her daughter's life:

> *"To this day," Michelle said, "she still will not admit she did anything wrong."*

Unfortunately, Michelle's experience is far from unique. Some parents intercept credit card applications meant for their adult children and then add themselves to the accounts. Others use their minor children's Social Security numbers to get utilities, cell phones, or new credit cards. Often, the crimes can continue for years before the victims have any clue what happened—or understand the price that they'll pay.

Like Michelle, Amy was in college when she discovered her mother had opened credit cards in Amy's name:

> *"At the time, I had threatened to go to the authorities, but I was talked out of it by my father," Amy said.*

It wasn't until Amy finished graduate school and tried to get an apartment and a car that she began to realize the full extent of the damage.

The crimes have created a "permanent rift" in Amy's family and left her feeling betrayed, violated, and isolated:

"For years I was ashamed of this and never spoke up when family members believed…the stories [my mother] told of our estrangement," Amy said.

Parental thieves put their victims into a horrific bind in other ways. Many creditors won't drop a fraudulent account unless the victim files a police report, which could result in the arrest and prosecution of the parent. Few children are willing to take that step.

Katie finally did after being repeatedly victimized by her mother. The older woman first drained Katie's credit union account, and then she applied for utilities in Katie's name:

"At that time, I didn't really know what to do," Katie said. *"No one I knew had ever been in that situation."*

It wasn't until Katie and her husband applied for a mortgage, and two more fraudulent accounts appeared on Katie's credit report, that she finally took action:

"I got the police report, spoke to three different lawyers about what I should do, contacted each credit bureau and collection agency," Katie said. *"Two of the three accounts have been taken off my record. I'm still waiting to hear about the third account."*

Katie's mom hasn't been arrested, but Katie has little faith that the experience has changed the older woman:

"I really am worried that this will happen again in the future," to Katie or to someone else, Katie said. *"She will find someone to latch on to and use them until they find out about it."*

What to Do if the Credit Bureau Won't Budge

Kay in Valley View, Texas, lost her adult daughter seven years ago to a blood clot. Wanting to do the right thing, Kay paid off a loan she'd cosigned with her daughter.

Ever since then, however, the three credit bureaus all list Kay as "deceased." Kay's credit file has been mixed with that of her daughter's, and as a result, Kay can't get credit:

> *"I have no FICO score," Kay wrote. "I have tried and tried to get it changed. Several times I sent [the bureaus] copies of phone bills, electric bills, Social Security papers, driver's license, on and on, everything I've been asked to send. [It's] still not resolved."*

It shouldn't be that hard to prove you're alive, or correct any other mistake in your credit file, for that matter. But sometimes, it is. If you've followed the suggestions in this book and are still slamming into a brick wall, you might need to take extraordinary measures.

Here's what can help:

- **Get stubborn**—Many people are appalled at the amount of time and energy it can take to get the simplest problem solved. Those who are tenacious to the point of obsession are in the best position to wear the opposition down. The bureaus, creditors, and collection agencies are counting on you to go away after a few rebuffs; credit-repair veterans say they often win their cases by repeatedly refusing to take "no" for an answer.

- **Consult with those who have gone before**—The best tactics for winning the battle change constantly as all sides adjust their strategies. Check out credit repair sites such as CreditBoards.com, which can give you some ideas and strategies from people who have some experience fighting the same battles. Just remember to take everything you read with a grain of salt—anyone can post on these boards.

- **Get a lawyer's help**—It's not easy to find a good attorney who's up on the nuances of the Fair Credit Reporting Act and the Fair Debt Collection Practices Act. But they're out there. Again, you can get referrals from your local bar association, legal aid office, or the National Association of Consumer

Advocates at www.naca.net. Even if your lawyer isn't cracker-jack, the other side might take you more seriously if correspondence about your case suddenly starts coming on the letterhead of Willgetya, Butgood, & Howe.

- **Get Congress involved**—Many people are surprised to learn that their U.S. representative is willing to weigh in on consumer issues, and most maintain a staff to help their constituents. Don't expect your elected representative to get excited about aiding your campaign to delete a $99 collection from your credit report. But if your story has any outrage factor at all—why can't the bureaus figure out you're alive, or not your father, or the victim of identity theft?—you might be able to enlist his help.

- **Call a local newspaper, television, or radio reporter**—Most media outlets have someone who covers finance or consumer issues. An ongoing battle with a credit bureau can be a juicy story, if told correctly. Be as succinct as you can when contacting the reporter (by email is usually best). If you don't get a response, follow up politely in a few weeks to ask whether they can refer you to anyone else.

You'll probably have the best luck at a smaller newspaper, station, or Web site. Reporters and columnists at large outlets get so many of these sad stories that they can follow up on only a fraction of the leads. Like the big regulators, they usually wait for a pattern of specific abuses to develop before they act, so your letter might or might not ever get answered. That doesn't mean you shouldn't try, but if you get no response, aim for a smaller media outlet closer to home.

9

Emergency! Fixing Your Credit Score Fast

If you've read this far, you know what a tedious process fixing errors on your credit report can be.

Credit bureaus have 30 days to investigate complaints and often defer to what lenders say about you, regardless if it's true. Even if all parties agree that a mistake has been made, the errors can continue to crop up in your files thanks to the automated nature of most credit reporting. You might have to contact creditors and the bureaus several times to get inaccuracies deleted. The process might take weeks; at worst, you might be fighting the battle for months or even years.

If you're in the midst of trying to get a mortgage, these errors can cause serious problems. You might not have enough time to fix your report before the house falls out of escrow or you get stuck with an interest rate much higher than you deserve to pay.

Troubles such as these might tempt you to turn to one of the many companies that promise "instant credit repair" or that guarantee to boost your credit score. No legitimate company makes such promises or guarantees, though, so anyone who hires one of these outfits is begging to be scammed.

There are, however, a growing number of genuine services that can fix mistakes on your credit report in 72 hours or less. Read on to learn more.

Repairing Your Credit in a Matter of Hours: Rapid Rescoring

Rapid rescoring services came about because too many people were losing loans or paying too much interest because of credit bureau inaccuracies. Before you get excited, though, you should learn what these services can and can't do:

- **They can't deal with you directly as a consumer**—Rapid rescoring is typically offered by small credit-reporting agencies, which serve as a kind of middleman between the bureaus and the lending professionals.

  These agencies, which are often independent but might be subsidiaries of credit bureaus, provide special services for loan officers and mortgage brokers such as merged or "3-in-1" credit reports. To benefit from rapid rescoring, you need to work with a loan officer or mortgage broker who subscribes to an agency that offers the service.

- **They can help you only if you have proof, or if proof can be obtained**—Rapid rescoring services aren't designed to help people who have yet to start the credit-repair process. You need something in writing, such as a letter from the creditor acknowledging that your account was reported as late when you were in fact on time. (This is one of the reasons that it's so important to get everything in writing when you're trying to fix your credit.) If you don't have such proof, but the creditor has acknowledged the error, some rapid rescorers can get the proof for you. However, that might add days or weeks to the process.

- **They can help you get errors fixed, but they can't remove true negative items that are in dispute**—Again, you need proof that a mistake was made—not just your say-so. If the credit bureau is already investigating your complaint about an error, the item typically can't be included in a rapid rescoring process.

- **They can't promise to help your score**—As you read in Chapter 2, "How Credit Scoring Works," sometimes removing negative items can actually hurt a score—strange as that might seem.

The scoring formula tries to compare you to people who have similar credit histories. If you've been lumped into the group with a bankruptcy or other black marks on your report, you might find that your score *falls* when some of those negative items are removed. Instead of being at the top of the bankrupts' group, in other words, you've dropped to the bottom of the next group—the folks who have better credit.

More commonly, removing an error might not help your score as much as you might have hoped and might not win you a better interest rate. There are no guarantees with rapid rescoring.

But Doug in Phoenix is one of the many borrowers who have benefited so far. Doug filed for bankruptcy in 1998, but several of his wiped-out debts were still shown as open and unpaid on his credit report five years later when he applied for a mortgage.

Technically, all the accounts should have been reported as "included in bankruptcy." It's a common enough error, and one that can usually be fixed—if you have a month or more.

Doug didn't. He worried that he would lose the house he wanted to buy and perhaps miss out on some of the lowest rates borrowers had seen in years. Doug's mortgage broker used his bankruptcy papers to prove the errors to a rapid rescoring service, which fixed the problems and boosted Doug's score.

The rate he got—just over 7 percent—was still higher than someone who had good credit would have received at the time, but it was much better than the rate he might have received without the fix.

This is exactly the kind of intervention that the National Association of Mortgage Brokers was hoping for when it began lobbying in 1997 for a way to speed up the dispute process and keep old, proven errors from killing mortgage deals. Congress had made some updates to the Fair Credit Reporting Act in 1996 that were supposed to help consumers, but the problems remained widespread.

Once upon a time, brokers and other lending professionals could do something about these problems. In the days before the widespread use of a credit score, a broker or loan officer could intervene to convince a lender to ignore mistakes or small blemishes on a client's credit file. Everyone involved understood that credit report errors were common, and having an experienced loan pro vouch for your creditworthiness could often get a deal done.

With the advent of credit scoring and automated loan processes, though, those opportunities to advocate for clients quickly evaporated. Lending professionals shared consumers' frustration when erroneous information continued to be reported by the bureaus—information that often dampened credit scores and resulted in worse rates and terms than the borrower deserved.

The mortgage brokers wanted a way to cut through the bureaucracy and speed up the process. Independent credit reporting agencies, with their smaller, specialized staffs, began to fill the need.

Here's how it works. Your loan officer or broker collects proof from you that a mistake has been made, and he transmits that proof to the credit agency that provides the rapid rescoring service.

The rescorers, in turn, have special relationships with the credit bureaus that allow their requests to be processed quickly. The rescoring service sends proof of errors to special departments at the credit bureaus, and the departments contact the creditors (usually electronically). If the creditor agrees that an error was made, the bureaus quickly update your credit report. After that happens, a new credit score can be calculated.

The cost for this service is typically somewhere between $30 and $45 for each "trade line" or account that's corrected. However, some agencies provide the rescoring for no extra charge, as part of a package of services provided to lending professionals.

The availability of rapid rescoring doesn't change the fact that you need to be proactive about your credit. Months before applying for any loan, you need to order copies of your reports and start challenging any inaccuracies. You also need to keep your correspondence about these errors. After all, rapid rescorers typically require some kind of paper trail to follow to prove to the bureau that the mistakes indeed exist.

If you find yourself in the middle of getting a mortgage and an old problem recurs, rapid rescoring can help you get rid of the problem and save the deal. So, how do you find one of these services?

If you're already dealing with a loan officer or mortgage broker, ask whether she has access to a rapid rescoring service. If your lending pro has never heard of rapid rescoring, ask her to contact the agency that provides her company with credit reports to see if it's available.

Kyle, a mortgage consultant from Chicago, learned about rapid rescoring from an article I wrote and emailed me for suggestions on how to find such a service. It turned out that the agency that his company used for credit reports had long provided rescoring—Kyle just didn't know it.

What if you're not in the market for a mortgage, or otherwise don't qualify for rapid rescoring, but you still want quick results?

You'll have to redefine your definition of *quick,* for starters. Few things are rapid in credit repair. The following techniques typically won't show results in 72 hours, but you might see a noticeable bounce in your score in 30 to 60 days.

Boosting Your Score in 30 to 60 Days

Rebuilding your credit can be an agonizingly slow process, but you can take a few shortcuts that may increase your score in as little as a month or two, as discussed in the following sections.

Pay Off Your Credit Cards and Lines of Credit

One of the fastest ways to boost a score is to lower your *debt utilization ratio*—the difference between the amount of revolving credit that's available to you and the amount that you're using.

One simple way to improve your ratio is to redistribute your debt. If you have a big balance on one card, for example, you could transfer at least some of the debt to other cards. It's typically better for your scores to have small balances on a number of cards than a big balance on a single card.

You also could investigate getting a personal installment loan with your local credit union or bank, and use the money to pay down your cards. Applying for the loan may ding your scores a bit, but that's likely to be more than offset by the improvement to your scores from reducing the balances on your credit cards. (Credit scoring formulas are much more sensitive to the balances on revolving debt, such as credit cards, than to the balances on installment loans.)

A riskier strategy might be to take out a 401(k) loan. These loans don't show up on your credit report, but you do face a big hazard: If you lose your job, you typically have to pay the money back quickly or you'll incur taxes and penalties on the balance. If you decide to take a 401(k) loan, make sure you can repay the loan quickly to minimize the risk.

Whatever you do, don't cash out a 401(k) or withdraw money from an IRA to pay off credit card debt. A few points' difference on your credit score is not worth the short- and long-term costs you'll pay for a premature withdrawal.

Although moving debt around can lift your scores, the best strategy for your numbers and your finances long-term is to pay off revolving debt—either out of your current income, using cash that's sitting in a savings account, or selling stocks or other investments, as long as they aren't in a retirement account.

Use Your Credit Cards Extremely Lightly

Remember: The scoring formula likes to see a big gap between your balances and your limits—and it doesn't care whether you pay off your balances in full every month or carry them from month to month. What matters is how much of your credit limits you're actually using at any given time.

Some people insist they've boosted their scores by paying off their cards in full a few days before their statement closes. If their credit card issuers usually send out bills around the 25th, for example, these folks check their balances online about a week before and pay off whatever's owed, plus a few bucks to cover any charges that might crop up before the 25th. By the time the bills are actually printed, their balances are pretty close to zero. (If you use this technique, just make sure you make a second payment after your statement arrives if your balance isn't already zero. That will make sure you don't get dinged with late charges—and yes, that can happen, even though you made a payment earlier in the month.)

An easier way to keep your balances down is simply to pay cash for most purchases in the three months or so before you plan to get a loan.

Focus on Correcting the Big Mistakes on Your Credit Reports

If someone else's bankruptcy, collections, or charge-offs show up on your report, you will benefit by having those removed. If an account you closed is reported as open, however, you'll probably want to leave it alone. Having an account reported as "closed" on your file can't help your score and might hurt it.

Don't ignore a collection just because it's small or it's listed as paid off. These are serious negative marks that can significantly depress a credit score. But don't get too upset if the credit bureaus list the wrong employer or misspell your middle name. The credit scoring formula doesn't even consider these minutiae.

Use the Bureaus' Online Dispute Process

Some credit-repair veterans swear they get quicker results this way, but you still need to make printouts of everything you send to the bureaus and every communication you receive from them.

See if You Can Get Your Creditors to Report or Update Positive Accounts

As you've read, not all creditors report to all three bureaus, and some don't report consistently. If you can get a creditor to report an account that's in good standing, though, you might see an immediate bump in your score.

Darren of New York had a great FICO score with Experian but only fair scores with Equifax and TransUnion. The reason? Most of his credit history was with a single credit union, and that credit union reported only to Experian:

"Since mortgage lenders [use] the middle score," Darren said, "I am not getting the best deal because that is not an accurate score."

The middle score doesn't reflect Darren's full credit history.

Darren hasn't been able to convince his credit union to report to the other two bureaus. That means he's pretty much back to slow-lane solutions, such as getting a credit card or installment loan from a lender that reports to all three bureaus and making on-time payments.

What Typically Doesn't Work

There's a lot of folklore out there about how to fix a credit report fast. Most of it is bogus, such as what's outlined in the next sections.

Disputing Everything in Sight

Some of the phony credit-repair places blitz credit bureaus with disputes about anything and everything. In the past, this might have been temporarily effective if the credit bureaus removed the disputed items while they investigated. These days, though, the bad stuff typically stays on your file during the investigation, so you don't even get a temporary boost. Even when you do, most or all of the negative items simply come right back as soon as the original creditor confirms that they're correct. What might not come back are the accounts that are helping your score. The creditors might not bother to respond to the bureaus' requests for confirmation, and you could end up making matters worse.

Disputing too many items at once is also a good way to convince credit bureaus that you're filing "frivolous" disputes, and they might refuse to investigate at all.

To be on the safe side, don't dispute more than three or four negative items at once, unless (like Doug's bankruptcy accounts) your disputes are related. And don't pay anyone a fat fee to do this for you.

Creating a "New" Credit Identity

This is another favorite of scam artists. They might have you use a dead infant's Social Security number or tell you to apply for a taxpayer identification number, which the IRS typically issues to businesses.

Even if you do manage to pull off this fraud, you're left with an absolutely empty credit file. If you think it's hard to get loans when you have troubled credit, just try getting credit with no history at all. It could be years before you qualify for decent rates and terms, and by then all the negative marks you were so worried about would have either fallen off your original credit report or become so old that they would hardly affect your score.

Closing Troublesome Accounts

You can't get negative marks to fall off any quicker by closing accounts, and you might wind up seriously dinging your credit score.

Delinquencies, charge-offs, collections, and other negative marks can remain on your credit report for seven years, whether or not the original account is still open; bankruptcies can stay there for ten years.

Even if you've had problems with an account, it might still be having a positive influence on your credit score. If it's one of your older accounts, it could be helping to make your credit history look nice and long—remember, older is better when it comes to credit scoring. If it's a revolving account, the credit limit is factored into your overall debt utilization ratio. If you close the account, you could make your existing balances look larger while making your credit history look younger than it is.

10

Insurance and Your Credit Score

Tawny had been a loyal Allstate customer for 15 years. The Texas woman had paid her premiums on time and had never gotten a ticket, had an accident, or filed a claim.

Then her auto insurance premium tripled:

"I went through a devastating divorce where I lost my home and credit,"
said Tawny, who became a single mother with three small children.
"About a year later, I got a notice from Allstate that my auto insurance
rate was increasing…. I wasn't too worried until I got my first bill. I went
from paying $396 every six months to $1,200."

Kyra in Bridgeport, Connecticut, never had trouble with her auto insurer. But when she tried applying for a renter's insurance policy with MetLife, she was denied:

"Although I have some previous credit problems, I would have never guessed in a million years that I would be denied a $200-per-year renter's insurance policy based on my credit history," Kyra steamed. "I'm self-employed, educated, and a productive citizen. I'm not any more likely to file an insurance claim than an unemployed individual with a high credit score."

Glen in El Paso got a notice that his auto premium was being raised to $125 a month, from $85. After getting the runaround from his insurer, he discovered the reason wasn't bad credit—it was too much credit:

"My wife had opened a GAP department store credit card with a $500 limit, and used it," Glen said. "Nothing more."

Glen was told by his insurer that consumers who use more than half their available credit on a department store card "are considered high risk and therefore must pay higher rates."

John in Negley, Ohio, was recently notified that his homeowner's insurance premium would soar because of a recently filed bankruptcy. His only question for me: "Is this legal?"

That's typically one of the first questions many people have when informed that an insurer has raised their rates or denied them coverage based on their credit.

Here's the other question they understandably raise: What does my credit have to do with anything when it comes to insurance?

"My circumstances forced me into bankruptcy…. I've never had an accident in my life," said Chestena in Texas, who a year after her bankruptcy was quoted auto rates that were $400 to $2,000 higher than what she paid before she filed. "Poor credit does not mean that you are a risk or that you are prone to accidents."

Insurers, though, think otherwise. They believe credit is an excellent predictor of whether you'll file a claim—better, in fact, than almost any other factor, including your previous driving history.

What's more, using credit for insurance decisions is not only legal in most states, it's also the norm. The vast majority of property casualty insurers—those who provide auto and homeowners policies—use credit-based insurance scores in their underwriting.

Insurance scoring was slower to take hold in Canada, but by 2010, more than half of Canadian insurers used the scores.

The way insurers use credit information, however, can differ markedly from the way lenders use the same data. That's why some people who have good credit scores and would qualify for the best rates and terms from most lenders still wind up paying higher premiums.

History of Using Credit Scores to Price Insurance Premiums

Insurers have actually been using credit information since at least 1970, when the Fair Credit Reporting Act first sanctioned the practice. Lamont Boyd, who became a Fair Isaac executive, remembers his days reviewing credit reports as a young insurance underwriter in the 1970s.

Boyd says his job was to look for "clearly 'bad' signals," such as bankruptcies, foreclosures, or collections, which would be used as a reason to turn down the customer who was applying for insurance.

The process, according to Boyd and Fair Isaac, was subjective and inconsistent—much like the human-powered lending decisions being made in much of the credit industry at the time. People who might have been good risks, despite a few blemishes, were being turned down, whereas those who might have been worse risks were being accepted.

Fair Isaac decided to tackle the insurance market in the late 1980s, shortly after introducing the first credit scores based on credit bureau information. Although the company doesn't dominate insurance scoring the way that it does credit scoring, Fair Isaac has been instrumental in promoting the idea that credit information can give insurers an edge in predicting losses.

Fair Isaac introduced its first credit-based insurance score in 1991, and it hired actuarial consultants Tillinghast-Towers Perrin to review Fair Isaac's in-house studies of the links between credit history and insurance losses.

The correlations were so strong, said Tillinghast principal Wayne Holdredge, that the consultants were suspicious:

"We went back to the companies [that supplied the insurance data] and made them sign affidavits, saying that they hadn't cooked the books," Holdredge remembered. "Now the correlation is well understood, but back then it wasn't."

The cause of credit-based insurance scoring got another boost in 2000, when MetLife actuary James E. Monaghan published a study that matched 170,000 auto policies to the credit histories of the drivers.

Over and over, Monaghan found a correlation between black marks on credit reports and higher loss ratios for insurers. (A loss ratio measures how much an insurer pays out in claims for each dollar collected in premiums.)

Loss ratios rose steeply, for example, with the number of collection accounts appearing on a driver's record. Those who had no collection accounts cost the insurers an average of 74.1 cents for each dollar collected. Drivers who had one collection account had 97.5 cents in claims for each premium dollar collected, whereas those who had three or more collections cost insurers about $1.19.

Collection Accounts	Loss Ratio
None	74.1%
1	97.5%
2	108.4%
3 or more	118.6%

Monaghan found similar patterns with derogatory public records such as bankruptcies, liens, repossessions, foreclosures…

Derogatory Public Records	Loss Ratio
None	73.8%
1	96.5%
2	104.2%
3 or more	114.1%

…with delinquencies…

Account Status	Loss Ratio
No lates	72.2%
At least one late	92.3%

…and with debt utilization, or how much of available credit was in use…

Leverage Ratio	Loss Ratio
1%–10%	64.3%
11%–39%	70.9%
40%–60%	75.2%
61%–80%	81.2%
80%–100%	88.1%
101%+	96.6%

Correlations were a bit less linear for other credit information, such as inquiries, age of the consumer's oldest account, and amounts past due...

Amount Past Due	Loss Ratio
$0	70.20%
$100 to $199	95.9%
$200 to $499	92.7%
$500 to $999	107.2%
$1,000 to $2,000	97.2%
$2,000 to $5,000	100.5%
$5,000 to $10,000	106.1%
$10,000+	99.8%

...but the links were still strong enough to suggest a definite relationship between how well people handled their credit and how much they cost their insurers.

Monaghan's status as an industry insider, of course, led many consumer advocates to question his results. An independent study by the University of Texas at Austin a few years later, however, found similar patterns and a "statistically significant" link between credit scores and auto losses.

The UTA researchers matched credit scores to 153,326 auto policies issued in early 1998 and tracked which policies made claims in the ensuing 12 months:

"The lower a named insured's credit score, the higher the probability that the insured will incur losses on an automobile insurance policy," the UTA researchers said, "and the higher the expected loss on the policy."

The average loss per policy during the period was $695, but drivers who had the lowest credit scores cost their insurers $918, whereas those with the highest scores cost $558.

An even larger study of two million auto and homeowner's policies was conducted by the Texas Department of Insurance. That study found a similar strong link between credit scores and claims.

But What's the Connection?

What none of the studies have proven is a *causal* link between credit and claims. In other words, they can't explain why poor credit should lead to more insurance losses.

Insurers speculate that people who are responsible with their credit might be more likely to be responsible with their cars and homes. Or perhaps people who mismanage their finances are more likely to make claims because they need the cash.

MetLife's Monaghan, like others in the insurance industry, believes no one will ever say for certain why the two are linked. He points out that it's impossible to prove a causal link for most factors used in insurance decisions.

The fact that you've been in an accident in the past, for example, doesn't cause you to have another accident. But most people can accept the idea that someone who has already had an accident or two might be more likely to have another one. It makes sense, in a way that using credit history for insurance does not.

The lack of a clear, logical link isn't the only thing that concerns consumer advocates about insurance scoring. Among the leading critics of insurance scoring is Birny Birnbaum, a former Texas insurance commissioner who believes insurance scoring might be illegally discriminating against low-income people and minorities.

Birnbaum doesn't believe the UTA study was rigorous enough to determine whether it's really credit, rather than some other factor, that correlates with insurer losses. He fears credit is actually some kind of proxy for a factor that insurers wouldn't otherwise be allowed to use, such as ethnic background or income.

In fact, the Texas insurance department study found that black, Hispanics, and lower-income populations had worse-than-average credit scores, which meant they were getting worse-than-average rates from many insurers, regardless of their claims history, driving record, or other factors.

Insurers insist that their use of credit scoring is actuarially sound and not discriminatory. Persistent concerns about fairness, though, have led a few states to ban credit scoring by insurers, whereas others have imposed restrictions on how insurance companies can use credit information. Several states have adopted model legislation crafted by the National Conference of Insurance Legislators to regulate and restrict the use of credit. Among other things, the model legislation does the following:

- Forbids insurers from using credit information to deny, cancel, or fail to renew a policy

- Prevents insurers from using a consumer's lack of a credit history as a factor in determining premiums or coverage

- Requires insurers to review their credit-related decisions within 30 days if it turns out those decisions were based on erroneous credit reports

Critics say the legislation does more to legitimize insurance scoring than protect consumers, but others say the laws at least provide insurers with some curbs.

Consumers already had some protections, theoretically, under the Fair Credit Reporting Act. The act requires insurers to notify consumers if credit information has affected a policy decision in any way, and include the following in the notification:

- The reasons for the insurer's decision

- The bureau from which the credit information was obtained

- Instructions on how the consumer can get a credit report

If my mailbag is any indication, some insurers aren't doing a good job of following the law.

Glen, the man in El Paso whose insurance increased because of his wife's GAP card, played a long game of cat-and-mouse with his insurer when he asked why his rates had been hiked:

"My insurance agent passed me to corporate [headquarters]. Corporate threw up their hands and claimed it wasn't their fault, it's how [the company's score provider] scores my credit. I ask, how do they score it? They replied that I could only get this information from [the score provider]," Glen recounted in an email.

"[The score provider] won't answer the phone. You have to write in. I did. [The score provider's] answer was, 'It must be your credit report or your driving record.' I got both. Driving record perfect. Credit report even better than when I first got insurance.

"Finally [I] get a number to call. [The score provider said it] scores your credit according to how the insurance company wants them to. The insurance company then says they can't discuss the criteria [because] it's proprietary."

Glen said he finally pressured "someone at my insurance company to pressure someone at [the score provider] for an answer," which is when he learned that a maxed-out department store card was the culprit.

Clearly, it shouldn't be that hard to get answers.

Other readers have told me they called insurers for quotes, only to later find an inquiry by the insurance company on their credit reports. They say they weren't told a credit check would be run or given an explanation of how the information might affect their premium.

Even fans of insurance scoring admit that insurers sometimes fumble the ball. Boyd, Fair Isaac's point man on insurance scoring, agrees that many insurers aren't adequately explaining what they're doing. Customers are left baffled, as are the insurance agents who have the most contact with clients:

> *"The insurance companies have not done a good job educating their front-line agents to explain what's happening [to their customers]," Boyd said.*

Adding to the confusion is a market that's even more splintered than the credit-scoring market. Fair Isaac sells its model to more than 300 insurers, but the biggest companies either have their own custom insurance scores or use the LexisNexis Attract score.

Many people who have good credit scores, for example, have been told by their insurers that their rates increased because of their attempts to get credit.

If the insurer were using Fair Isaac's score, too many inquiries might at worst cause the customer to miss out on the insurer's best discounts, Boyd said. The consumer would still enjoy a break on premiums because of good credit, he said—it just might not be the best discount available.

If the insurer were raising everyone's rates by 15 percent, a customer who had a few too many inquiries might be charged 10 percent more, whereas the insurer's highest-rated customers might pay 5 percent more—and its worst-rated customers 20 percent more.

But Boyd couldn't vouch for how an insurer's custom score might treat inquiries, and the insurers who use custom scoring say such details are proprietary information.

Furthermore, you don't have a right to see the score that's being used to judge you, as you often do with credit decisions. You've long had a right to see the scores used in mortgage lending decisions; starting in July 2010, lenders have been required to reveal the scores they use when you don't get the best rates and terms. Insurers, however, aren't required to fess up.

Insurers are doing themselves no service by failing to explain the rules to their customers—particularly those who have good credit. As Boyd notes, someone who has bad credit might just accept a high premium as fate, but someone who has good credit is likely to react badly, even if they're just being shut out of the insurer's top tier of customers:

"Instead of getting an A, they got an A–," Boyd said, "and they're the ones who are going to start asking questions."

Insurers insist that credit-based scoring helps more people than it hurts. They say responsible policyholders pay less for their coverage than those who are more likely (in the insurers' view) to file a claim.

Indeed, some of the people who have written to me about their insurance scoring experience had happy news:

"I've been working hard on paying down debt and just bought a house this year," wrote Christopher of Lancaster, Pennsylvania. "About four months ago, I got my new insurance premium bill in the mail and noticed that it was significantly cheaper than what I was paying before. Nothing had changed but my credit rating.... This was confirmed by my State Farm agent. [Insurance scoring] is a good thing."

What Goes into an Insurance Score

It's hard to be definitive about what does and doesn't affect your insurance score. Many big insurers have their own credit-based scoring models, and they're not talking much about how those work. Fair Isaac is talking some, but its formula doesn't dominate the insurance-scoring world the way its credit score does the lending world.

But some information is better than nothing, and Fair Isaac is willing to share some of the details of what goes into its insurance-scoring model. The factors used are similar to the ones considered with credit scoring, although their weight can vary:

- Forty percent of the average insurance score is determined by payment history—whether you've paid your bills on time. That compares to 35 percent for the credit-scoring model. As with credit scoring, the model looks at your payment history on different types of accounts, including credit cards and installment loans. Black marks such as delinquencies, charge-offs, collections, foreclosures, repossessions, liens, and judgments can seriously affect your score.

- Thirty percent of your insurance score is based on your credit utilization, which is roughly the same percentage that your credit score uses. The score factors in the amount you owe on all of your accounts and how that compares to your credit limit (in the case of a credit card) or the amount you originally borrowed (for an installment loan).

- Fifteen percent of an insurance score has to do with the types of new credit you've been granted recently—how many new accounts you have, how long it's been since you opened a new account, and the number and type of inquiries on your report. By contrast, about 10 percent of the credit-scoring model is derived from the number and types of new credit you've acquired.

- Ten percent of the insurance score is based on the length of time you've had credit—which counts for about 15 percent of your credit score. Both scores factor in the age of your oldest account and the average age of all your accounts.

- Five percent of your insurance score measures types of credit in use, compared to 10 percent of your credit score. Once again, Fair Isaac is looking for that "healthy mix" of different types of credit, without providing much guidance about how many of each type of account you should have.

As you can see, Fair Isaac's insurance-scoring model puts slightly more emphasis on your payment history and your recent behavior in applying for new credit. The age of accounts and their mix are slightly less important.

Keeping a Lid on Your Insurance Costs

The strategies you're learning in this book will help you improve and protect your credit, which should, in turn, help you to qualify for lower insurance rates in most states.

Good credit alone, however, isn't enough to keep you from overpaying for insurance. You need to be smart about the kinds of coverage you buy and how you use that coverage.

Whether your credit is good or bad, consider the steps outlined in the next sections to control your insurance costs.

Start Thinking Differently About Insurance

Many people feel somehow ripped off if they pay their premiums for years without ever making a claim. But this is exactly what you *want* to happen.

Insurance is meant to protect you against the kind of big expenses that could wipe you out financially—not to pay for the little stuff you could easily cover out of your own pocket.

So if you're using insurance properly and you never make a claim, that means you've never suffered a major catastrophe. Who among us wouldn't like to get through life without having a car totaled, a house burn down, or a lawsuit filed against us?

People who don't understand the role of insurance often try to shift as much risk as possible to their insurer—by choosing low deductibles, for example, or making claims for every little ding their cars suffer in supermarket parking lots. That's a quick road to higher premiums.

In fact, making a lot of claims—or making even one of the wrong kind of claim, as you'll see later—can make it difficult for you to get coverage at all. Insurers share claims information and are on the lookout for people who are likely to cost them money. People who constantly turn to insurers to pay for damage they could have covered themselves often find fewer and fewer companies willing to insure them, and those companies are charging more and more to do so.

Does this seem unfair? If you think it does, you would expect to get some support from J. Robert Hunter, a consumer advocate and insurance expert for the Consumer Federation of America. He's been sharply critical of the insurance industry on many occasions, and he's seen by many reporters as the "go-to guy" when they need a succinct quote damning some bit of insurer foul play against consumers.

But Hunter, an insurance actuary and former Texas insurance commissioner, also knows how insurance is supposed to work. He maintains high deductibles on all his personal insurance policies, and he urges others to do so, too. He sets aside the money he saves on premiums to pay for out-of-pocket expenses.

Rather than protest, realize that this is how the insurance game is meant to be played. Preserve your coverage for the big disasters, and you'll save in the long run.

Raise Your Deductibles

This is one of the fastest and smartest ways to save money on insurance—but many people balk.

Raising your deductible means you'll pay less every year in premiums. You're also less likely to make claims for piddling stuff—claims that would likely result in your rates being jacked up.

So, if you can, boost your deductibles to at least $500 and preferably $1,000 or more. Leave at least that much money in your savings account to cover the cost of any accidents, and you'll be money ahead in the long run.

Don't Make Certain Kinds of Claims

There's something else that insurance is not—and that's a maintenance fund for your house and other property.

Insurance is designed to cover sudden and unexpected losses, such as a fire. If damage happens that you could have foreseen and prevented, you're on the hook. Insurers expect you to inspect, maintain, and protect your property without their help.

So, if a storm tears shingles off your roof and the resulting leak ruins your dining room ceiling, your policy will probably pay for repairs. If your roof is just old and falling apart, though, you'll have to reroof and fix the water stains on your own dime.

Termite and rodent infestations are another frequent cause of damage that few insurers cover. They figure you should have noticed the little critters and had them exterminated long before they had a chance to ravage your home.

If you make a claim for such problems, you very likely won't get a dime. But the claim could still count against you when it's time to renew your insurance.

Okay, let's say that the damage is indeed "sudden and unexpected": The rubber hose on your washing machine breaks and floods your house. Surely you should make that claim, right?

Maybe not. Insurers are particularly paranoid about water-damage claims. They took a beating from an exploding number of mold-related claims, including some famous ones, such as the contention from former *Tonight* show regular Ed McMahon that his home's toxic mold killed his dog.

Insurers share their claims experience in a huge database called CLUE, for Comprehensive Loss Underwriters Exchange. Readers have told me that a single mention in the CLUE database is enough to blackball their home for years. Some say they didn't even make an actual claim, but simply asked their insurer for information.

Tami of Seattle asked a claims adjuster to evaluate what looked like damage to her bathroom floor. The adjuster determined that water splashing over the tub had seeped under the vinyl flooring sometime in the past, but that there was no current indication of moisture and the damage was entirely cosmetic:

> *"This was enough to have my house branded as 'water-damaged,'" Tami wrote. "When I tried to shop for a more reasonably priced homeowner's policy, I was told by my agent that it was impossible because no one is accepting new policies with a history of water damage. None of the six companies they represent would accept my house. I was also told that even if I entirely replaced the bathroom floor, it would have no effect on my policy status."*

Oh, and it gets worse. A few readers have told me they had trouble selling their homes because of past water-related claims. Insurance companies balked at writing policies on the home for the new buyers; without insurance, mortgage lenders won't approve a loan.

Is this entirely rational? Of course not. Insurers are overreacting, as they tend to do. Eventually, a few insurance companies will realize they're avoiding some good customers, more will follow, and the water-related stigma will ease.

The best course for policyholders for right now, though, is prevention— and silence. Among the things you should be doing

- Regularly inspect your home. Every few months, check your roof and foundation for leaks or standing water.

- Fix any leaks immediately.

- Replace hoses on older washing machines and dishwashers. Your plumber can point you to a type that's less likely to break.

- If you live in a cold climate, take steps to adequately insulate your pipes and prevent breakage.

If, despite your best efforts, you suffer water-related damage, seriously consider paying for repairs yourself if you possibly can, and avoid mentioning the incident to your insurer. Preventing the "water-damage" stigma from attaching to your home could leave you money ahead in the long run.

Be a Defensive Driver

A patrol officer once explained to me that there are few true "accidents" on the road, but many, many crashes.

What's the difference? *Accident* implies the collision was out of the control of at least one of the drivers involved. That's rarely the case. Although one driver might be the direct cause, many times the other drivers could have avoided the crash had they been driving more defensively.

Obviously, there are exceptions. One of my dear friends was killed when a tractor-trailer rig flew over a center divider and smashed into his car. There's not much he could have done to avoid this accident other than staying home that particular day.

In most crashes, however, all the drivers involved are at least partially at fault. If you've ever been hit, you can probably think of ways you could have avoided the collision. Maybe you were tailgating or driving too fast, not giving yourself enough time and road space to react. Or maybe you just weren't paying enough attention to what was going on ahead of you, or to the sides, or in your rear-view mirror. Who among us hasn't been distracted in a car by a child, a conversation, a cell phone, or a music player?

Driving is dangerous business, and we owe it to ourselves, our passengers, and our pocketbooks to give it our full attention.

Use the Right Liability Limits

This might not save you money in the short run, but it could help you if you ever cause a serious accident or get sued.

Liability coverage pays for the damage you cause (or are accused of causing) to other people and other people's property. If someone slips and falls in your house or suffers serious injuries in a car crash for which you're found to be at fault, they can sue you for everything you're worth—and then some.

That's why you want to have liability coverage on your home and cars that's at least equal to your net worth. Some insurance experts recommend having twice that amount, or even more for people who are "lawsuit targets"—doctors, lawyers, public figures.

If you need to buy more coverage than your insurer offers—liability coverage for autos and homes usually maxes out at $500,000—consider buying a separate "umbrella" or personal liability policy. These policies kick in after the liability limits on your auto or homeowner's insurance have been exhausted, and typically cost about $300 for $1 million of coverage.

Drop Collision and Comprehensive on Older Cars

Collision coverage pays for the damage you do to your own car in an accident, whereas comprehensive covers the other disasters that can happen—your car is stolen, dented in a hailstorm, or squashed by a falling tree branch.

This coverage is usually a good idea on newer cars and is sometimes required by your financing company. The older your car, though, the less likely you are to get much money from the insurer even if the worst happens.

If your car is stolen or totaled, your insurance company will send you a check for an amount that's usually somewhere between its trade-in value at a dealership and what it would be worth if you sold it yourself.

If you haven't checked the value of your car lately, you might be surprised at how small that check is likely to be. (Online sites like Edmunds.com or KBB.com, the Kelley Blue Book site, can clue you in.)

If your car is old enough that you'd just replace it with a new one, and you wouldn't have much trouble coming up with a down payment on that next car without your insurer's help, dropping comprehensive and collision is a no-brainer. There's something you need to know, however: If you don't have comprehensive and collision on your car, you likely won't have the coverage on a rental car, either. You might need to buy the rental company's (notoriously expensive) coverage, or see if your credit card offers "primary" coverage that would include it. Most credit cards that have rental car insurance offer only secondary coverage, which means they pay only what your insurance company doesn't. Some cards, including American Express, have optional coverage you can add to make the card your primary insurance. Call and ask your card issuer what's available.

Shop Around

This has always been important, but never more so now that credit is such a factor.

Insurers tend to set their rates based on their own experiences. That's why premiums for the same drivers and cars can vary by thousands of dollars from one insurance company to the next, even when credit isn't considered.

If your credit is mediocre or poor, you'll probably want to look for insurers that don't use credit information. There are still a number of these companies out there; they believe they've found other good ways to manage their risk.

You can look for an independent insurance agent who can tell you which companies don't use credit information, or simply call around and ask. Don't give out identifying details, like your name and Social Security number, until you're sure the company doesn't use credit info. (Like others who have a "legitimate business need," insurers are allowed to pull your credit reports without your permission. So if you don't want them to check your credit, don't give them the necessary details to do so.)

If your credit is decent, you shouldn't shy away from companies that use insurance scores, because you could benefit.

A good place to start shopping is often your state Department of Insurance, which might offer some kind of premium survey that can help you see which companies are most likely to offer you a good deal, given your location and situation. (These regulators also might provide complaint surveys, so you can avoid the insurers that create the most problems for their customers.) An auto insurer that has a good track record of managing the risks of teenage drivers, for example, is likely to give you and your 16-year-old a better rate than one that wants to steer clear of underage drivers.

You can also use quote services such as InsWeb.com or call the companies directly.

You may wonder how shopping for insurance will affect your credit or insurance score. Insurers typically say their models disregard any inquiries related to insurance. Still, for security and privacy reasons, you want to limit how many entities are peeking into your credit files. Narrow down the field of potential companies before you give any insurer enough details to pull your reports.

Protect Your Score

Although insurance scores are a bigger mystery, much of the same behavior that protects your credit score should help improve and maintain your insurance score. Those behaviors include the following:

- Paying your bills on time

- Keeping balances low on credit cards and lines of credit

- Not applying for credit you don't need

If you do need to open new accounts, try to do so after you've renewed your policies for the year.

11

Can Bad Credit Cost You a Job?

Lose your job, and you may have trouble paying the bills. Have trouble paying your bills, and you may find it tough to get a new job.

That Catch-22 is what many people face thanks to the widespread use of credit background checks. These checks have become routine among employers, even as soaring unemployment and foreclosures have resulted in black marks on millions of people's credit histories.

Approximately 50 percent of private employers check the credit histories of at least some of their job applicants, according to a survey by the Society for Human Resource Management.

Companies say they do so primarily to prevent or reduce crime, such as theft and embezzlement. The idea is that people who have debt problems are more likely to steal or commit other crimes.

The problem with this is that there is *absolutely no research supporting a connection between bad credit and bad morals*. A credit bureau spokesman admitted as much even as the bureaus were trying to persuade Oregon legislators that the reports still should be available to employers.

"At this point we don't have any research to show any statistical correlation between what's in somebody's credit report and their job performance or their likelihood to commit fraud," conceded Eric Rosenberg, the state government liaison for TransUnion credit bureau.

Despite the lack of evidence, TransUnion and other credit bureaus that provide the reports say they're an important tool for evaluating applicants.

Their arguments didn't work. The Oregon legislature passed a bill into law that prohibits employers in the state from using credit checks for hiring, firing, promoting, or determining compensation for most workers. Exceptions were made for financial institutions, public-safety officers, and when an employer can prove credit history is important to a job and a background check is disclosed to the applicant or employee.

Several states—including California, Colorado, Connecticut, Hawaii, Illinois, Maryland, Nevada, Oregon, Vermont, and Washington—have curbed widespread use of credit checks in making hiring decisions. Similar laws have been introduced into other states and Congress. Lawsuits have been filed over the practice as well, including one by the U.S. Equal Employment Opportunity Commission against Kaplan Higher Education Corp., a for-profit college company. The EEOC said Kaplan's use of credit histories "has an unlawful discriminatory impact because of race and is neither job-related nor justified by business necessity." Since African Americans and Latinos tend to have worse credit scores than whites or Asians, the use of credit checks has a disparate impact on those minorities and is a violation of the Civil Rights Act, the EEOC contended.

Those already employed aren't safe from credit checks, either—especially if they work for the federal government, which often requires good credit for various security clearances.

The federal Defense Finance and Accounting Service, which handles payroll for the military and the Pentagon, in 2010 fired dozens of long-time workers for bad credit after reclassifying their jobs into categories that imposed tighter requirements. Most of the workers were African American, leading Congressional representatives Dennis Kucinich and Marcia Fudge to denounce the action as discriminatory.

You don't even have to work directly for the government to be affected by its credit check policies. A reader named Gene worked for a consulting agency that was hired to do some work for the Internal Revenue Service in Philadelphia. Two months after he started the IRS job, a government investigator told him his poor credit was endangering his position.

"I was advised to clean up my credit report if I wanted to remain a consultant," Gene said. "They gave me a month. There's not a whole lot you can do to straighten up your credit in month."

Gene insisted his credit "wasn't that bad to begin with... no defaulted student loans or bankruptcies or anything like that." But four months after he was hired, Gene said his employer told him not to report to work anymore.

I didn't write about employer use of credit checks in the earliest editions of this book, because employers look at credit *reports*, not credit *scores*. But there's mounting evidence that employers are abusing credit checks, sometimes even violating federal law when they do so, and you need to know about the risks you face when you're trying to get a job.

The same human resources survey found:

- Thirteen percent of employers use credit checks for all their employees, including those who don't handle money, have any fiduciary or financial responsibilities, or even have access to sensitive information. There's no evidence credit checks are effective in preventing crime even in financially sensitive positions, so how can we justify them for anyone else?

- Many employers acknowledged that a bankruptcy on an applicant's credit report would most likely result in a decision not to make a job offer. Here's the problem: Using a bankruptcy as a decision not to hire (or to fire or to refuse a promotion) is illegal under federal law (Title 11 of the U.S. Code).

- A majority (64 percent) allows applicants to explain credit-check results before the final hiring decision is made. But 28 percent allow applicants to explain only after a decision is made, and 8 percent don't allow any explanation. Even if employers were convinced that credit checks prevent crime, why wouldn't they want to know if an applicant was the victim of identity theft or ran up debt for a life-saving operation for a child?

Employers' perception that there's a correlation between credit problems and problems on the job may not have a basis in reality, but another factor is driving this trend: fear of lawsuits. Employers don't want to be sued for negligent hiring if their employees do wrong, especially in businesses where workers have access to customers' money or possessions, such as banking, property management, hotel, and home health care industries. A client isn't likely to sue the visiting health care worker who steals her jewelry; instead, she might sue the employer, which is perceived as having deeper pockets and responsibility for hiring the thief.

"The employer will have a tough time defending itself," one labor attorney told me, "if it didn't take the simple measure of doing a background check."

Of course, there's a difference between a background check that includes criminal records and employment history, and one that includes a look at your credit.

If an employer does a credit check on you, it shouldn't be a surprise or done in secret. The federal Fair Credit Reporting Act requires employers to get your written permission to conduct the check on a document separate from the employment application.

I recently got this email from a job hunter:

"You once said in a column that employers sometimes check your credit report but that they had to let you know if that was a factor in denying you a job. I think employers routinely check credit reports and don't say anything to you about it," the job hunter wrote. "I have two master's degrees but am having trouble finding employment, and I think it's due to my credit, which is in the toilet at the moment. I don't see my situation getting any better unless I can get a job commensurate with my education and skills so I can start to repair things."

While it's possible secret credit checks are going on, it's somewhat unlikely. It costs employers money to run background checks, so they more often use other methods to winnow down the applicants when they have a deluge of applications—as many employers do when unemployment is high. At the time this reader wrote to me, there were six unemployed people for every available job opening.

If you are asked to give permission for a credit check, you don't realistically have much choice if you want the job. But you can take the opportunity to explain the circumstances of your bad credit to a potential employer, especially if the problems have been resolved, were the result of a mishap beyond your control, or could be fixed simply by you being employed again. Will it do any good? Maybe not, but it may be your one shot at salvaging your chances.

When employers do order credit checks, they may learn more about you than a creditor would. In most cases, for example, the FCRA says the following cannot be reported to employers or creditors:

- Bankruptcies after ten years.

- Civil suits and civil judgments, and records of arrest, from date of entry, after seven years.

- Paid tax liens after seven years.

- Accounts placed for collection after seven years.

- Any other negative information (except criminal convictions) after seven years. (Criminal convictions can be reported indefinitely, although some states have laws restricting how long they can be reported.)

But these reporting restrictions are waived when employers are doing background checks related to jobs with an annual salary of $75,000 or more a year.

Employment experts say "well-intentioned" employers typically won't reject you over a few minor slip-ups. They're looking for more serious problems such as collection actions, repossessions, foreclosures, and evictions. Some check the level of your debts against your current or past salaries to determine whether you're living beyond your means.

If an employer does use a background or credit check as a reason to deny you a job or a promotion, rescind a job offer, or fire you, you're entitled to see the evidence against you.

Before the adverse action is taken, the company must give you a "pre-adverse action disclosure," which includes a copy of the report and an explanation of your rights under the fair credit reporting laws.

Once the employer takes the adverse action, you're supposed to get another notice with the name, address, and phone number of the employment screening company and language informing you that you have the right to dispute the accuracy or completeness of its report.

Do all employers comply with the law? Probably not. Rather than go through all this, many employers find a less-complicated excuse to give you, or they simply do not give you a reason why you weren't hired.

Your right to dispute erroneous information is of limited use, anyway. The employer isn't required to wait while you try to fix erroneous information; it's perfectly free to give the job to someone else. Unless and until you're covered by laws that restrict credit checks in employment decisions, you'd be wise to take a proactive approach to what's being reported about you.

That means:

- Check your credit reports at least once a year at www.annual-creditreport.com and promptly dispute any serious errors.

- Pay for a background check on yourself if you'll be looking for another job. The check may turn up other errors, such as a criminal record that belongs to someone else.

- Contact your state and federal lawmakers if you're concerned about the growing trend of employers using credit checks.

12

Keeping Your Score Healthy

Mark from Seattle sent me a furious email after reading one of my columns about how to beef up a credit score.

Didn't I realize, he asked, that most of the strategies wouldn't work for someone who was out of a job, facing huge medical bills, and otherwise up to his ears in debt? How was he supposed to save his credit when he couldn't scrape together the cash to pay his rent?

Mark brings up a good point. All the score-enhancing strategies in the world won't help if you can't pay your bills.

For Mark and millions like him, bankruptcy might be the only real option—and a choice made by a huge number of people each year.

Even so, far fewer households opt for bankruptcy than could actually benefit from filing, according to economist Michelle J. White, currently of University of California, San Diego.

White studied bankruptcy filings in the mid-1990s, when consumer filings first hit the one million mark. She found that although about 1 percent of households were filing each year, 15 percent had finances in such poor shape that they would be better off financially by going bankrupt.

Even before the most recent recession, many families lacked the resources to financially survive the inevitable setbacks that life throws them—job loss, divorce, accidents, or illness. And not all these families subsisted below the poverty line. Many had good incomes, nice homes, and new cars, but they made no provision for the rainy days that come into everyone's lives.

In fact, the leading cause of bankruptcy is job loss combined with consumer debt and inadequate savings, according to comprehensive research by Jay L. Westbrook, Teresa A. Sullivan, and Elizabeth Warren, authors of *The Fragile Middle Class: Americans in Debt.* Medical bills, divorce, and burdensome mortgage debt are other key factors.

If you want to reduce the odds of becoming yet another statistic, you can take measures to help ensure that your score stays healthy. You might call them the three "do's" and five "don'ts" of bankruptcy proofing your life.

The Do's of Credit Health

The following actions can help you survive life's setbacks and keep you out of bankruptcy court. The idea is to increase your financial flexibility and to protect yourself against some of the bigger risks you might face.

Pay Off Your Credit Card Balances

If one lesson about credit could be taught to every schoolchild, it should be this.

Paying off your credit cards every month is a good way to ensure that you'll always live within your means. You'll have the flexibility to weather bad times and take advantage of good times if you're not carrying a credit card balance around.

You won't be paying thousands of dollars—and more likely, tens of thousands of dollars—in unnecessary interest during your lifetime.

Consider this. Someone who carries a $5,000 credit card balance will pay somewhere around $70 a month in interest. If she were to invest that money instead, it could grow to nearly $250,000 over her working lifetime, assuming an 8 percent average annual return. That's a pretty big price to pay for the convenience of not paying cash.

Credit card debt also plays a big role in bankruptcies and other financial catastrophes. The actual crisis might be caused by job loss, divorce, or other setbacks, but it's their heavy burden of credit card debt that usually causes people to file.

Carrying a balance also leaves you vulnerable to the various games that credit card companies play, such as these:

- Deciding your fixed rate is no longer fixed, and raising it going forward

- Raising your rate if you're 60 days late with a payment

- Chopping your credit limit, making your existing balances loom larger and potentially hurting your credit scores

The only winners in this game are the ones who don't play—who don't carry credit card balances from month to month and who never pay interest.

Despite what you might have heard, that's actually the norm in America.

Most American households have no credit card debt, according to the latest Federal Reserve study of consumer finances. About a quarter of American households have no credit cards, and another 37 percent regularly pay off their balances. Half of those who do carry some credit card debt owe $2,300 or less.

That statistic you might have heard, that "the average American owes more than $9,000 in credit card debt," is bogus. The numbers are typically created simply by dividing the total outstanding credit card debt by the number of American households with credit cards. This calculation doesn't factor in balances that are about to be paid off.

Using averages also can be misleading because a relative handful of consumers with huge credit card balances can skew the statistics.

It's kind of like measuring the "average" net worth of a group of 20 people when one of them is Warren Buffett. Even if the other 19 were stone cold broke, the "average" wealth of a person in that group would be about $2 billion.

On a less-extreme scale, that is what's happening with the credit card debt statistic. Federal Reserve statistics show that fewer than 1 in 20 households actually owes more than $10,000, but the big balances by those few households skew the average.

If you're one of those who thought you were "average" in carrying credit card debt, realize you're not—and get ahead by leaving the debt behind.

Have an Emergency Fund

Americans' lack of rainy-day funds is epidemic. Only one in four households in recent Bankrate.com polls had an emergency fund, and 62 percent could not pay an unexpected expense such as a $500 car repair from their savings or checking accounts.

That corresponds with findings by the National Bureau for Economic Research, which said nearly half of U.S. households are "financially fragile" and would be unable to cover an unexpected $2,000 expense.

Researchers used data from the 2009 TNS Global Economic Crisis survey, which asked, "If you were to face a $2,000 unexpected expense in the next month, how would you get the funds you need?" In the United States, 24.9 percent of respondents said they would be "certainly able" to cope, 25.1 percent said "probably able," 22.2 percent said "probably unable," and 27.9 percent said "certainly unable." The ways some people would cope with an unexpected bill gave researchers further pause. Nearly 19 percent of the respondents said they would sell or pawn possessions or take out a payday loan. Others would rely on loans from friends or credit cards.

Other researchers believe fewer than one in three U.S. households has sufficient savings to survive even a short (three-month) stretch of unemployment.

The reality is that scraping together an emergency fund takes a lot of work, but having one can be enormously freeing.

I was working for the *Anchorage Times* in Alaska when the venerable old paper announced one day that it was going out of business. We had less than 12 hours of notice. The announcement was made about 1:00 p.m., and the last edition rolled off the press around midnight.

People around me worried aloud about how they would pay their mortgages, their credit cards, and their child support. But when I went home and totaled the numbers, I realized I could live for six months on my savings without touching my retirement funds or altering my lifestyle all that much. If I made a few cutbacks, I could last a year.

The peace of mind I had that day, and in the month or so that it took to find my next reporting gig, is almost indescribable. Knowing that you can lose or walk away from any job is incredibly powerful. Of course, that was back before I had a mortgage or a child. But having bigger, built-in expenses just increases the need for having funds at the ready.

You might think that you don't make enough money to set aside a reserve, but people who have studied the issue have found that whether you save has relatively little to do with what you bring in.

Steven Venti of Dartmouth and David Wise of Harvard used Social Security lifetime earnings and net income assessments for 3,992 households whose heads were near retirement age. Here's what they found:

- Savings and wealth vary enormously at every income level. Many low-income households don't have anything saved, but that's also true of many high-earning families.

- Disparities in wealth can't be explained by income alone, because some of the lowest-earning households managed to build significant wealth.

- Income differences explained just 5 percent of the variations, and life events—inheritances, big medical bills, divorce, the number of children—accounted for just 4 percent of the dispersion. Investment choices accounted for another 8 percent.

In other words, the vast majority of the differences in wealth had nothing to do with income, life events, or how the money was invested.

What did make the difference? How much the families chose to save. Venti and Wise determined that those who had a goal of saving built wealth, regardless of their circumstances.

Saving isn't easy, and if you're busy paying down credit card debt, it also might not be your first priority. But, as a starter, try to keep at least $1,000 in cash handy. Toss in any tax refunds you get, and as soon as possible set up an automatic transfer so that the money is whisked from your paycheck to your emergency fund before you even see it.

You'd be wise to keep the money somewhere safe and accessible, such as an FDIC-insured savings account. For a while in the go-go years, it was fashionable to believe that people could put their emergency funds in the stock market and make great returns. The bear markets of 2000 and 2008 should have squashed that theory, but people still ask me how they can get better returns on their emergency funds. You really can't, if you want the money to be there when you need it. You don't want your fund to lose 50 percent or more of its value right when the economy is tanking and your boss decides that your job is now superfluous.

If you're a homeowner and have sufficient equity, you can consider opening a home equity line of credit as a stand-in for an emergency fund until you can get the appropriate amount saved. For this strategy to work, though, you have to leave the line unused. Don't be tempted to rack up more debt by borrowing needlessly against your home.

Have Adequate Insurance

Before the Affordable Care Act changed the rules, health insurance often was expensive and, for many people, tough to get. At one point, more than 45 million Americans were uninsured and medical bills were a factor in nearly two-thirds of personal bankruptcies filed in the United States, according to research by Harvard professor (and now U.S. Senator) Elizabeth Warren.

By contrast, medical bills are a negligible issue in Canada, which has universal health insurance. It's one of the reasons why Canada's bankruptcy rate prior to 2006 was less than one-third that of the United States.

The ACA, commonly known as Obamacare, made health insurance more attainable by offering subsidies to most taxpayers. The ACA also banned insurers from using pre-existing conditions to deny coverage or raise premiums, and required that children up to age 26 be allowed to remain on their parents' policies.

The ACA caused the largest drop in the number of uninsured since the creation of Medicare and Medicaid half a century earlier. Still, many people remain vulnerable because they still don't have insurance, or their insurance is inadequate.

Alana's policy required her to make 30 percent copayments—which was affordable when the Indianapolis woman sought routine care, but not when her daughter was born critically ill:

"My daughter... spent several weeks in intensive care. Add this to already maxed-out credit cards," Alana said, "and it was a recipe for disaster."

Alana wound up filing bankruptcy to wipe out thousands of dollars in doctor and hospital bills.

Some people who are young and healthy think they don't need coverage, but no one can predict when an accident or major illness might strike. If you have coverage through your employer, by all means take advantage of it. If you don't, check out your options at HealthCare.gov.

Your health isn't the only risk you need to insure. Take a look, too, at your liability coverage. This is the part of your homeowner's and auto insurance that protects you against lawsuits. Make sure your liability limits on each of your policies is at least equal to your total net worth.

I'd like to include a pitch for disability insurance, as well, if it's available through your employer. You're much more likely to be disabled and unable to work than you are to die before you retire, yet most people don't have a long-term disability plan. You can also try buying an individual policy, although these have become rather expensive in recent years.

The Don'ts of Credit Health

Building and protecting your financial resources is a good start, but equally important is limiting how much debt you incur in your lifetime.

Don't Buy More House Than You Can Afford

Skyrocketing foreclosure rates vividly demonstrated the dangers of stretching too far to buy a house. Yet even as lenders tightened their standards in the wake of the mortgage mess, it was still possible to borrow far more than you could comfortably repay. Mortgage payments used to be capped at 26 percent to 28 percent of your gross monthly income, but many lenders today still let homebuyers borrow up to 33 percent, and some go even higher.

Lenders know you probably will do whatever it takes to keep your home, even if it means short-changing your retirement, giving up vacations, and driving yourself deep into debt. Homeowners' desire to hang on to their houses despite "insurmountable debt," according to researchers Sullivan, Warren, and Westbrook, is a leading contributor in Chapter 13 bankruptcies.

Many homebuyers also underestimate all the ancillary costs of buying a home, such as maintenance, repairs, improvements, and decoration. At the same time, lenders are falling over themselves to extend you credit because homeowners are generally viewed as more stable and financially responsible than renters.

Lillian and her now ex-husband were actually conservative when they bought their first home, keeping their mortgage payments to just 20 percent of their gross income. The problems started immediately, though, as lenders rushed to give them money:

> *"It was heady to have so many offers of loans after we purchased our home," Lillian wrote. "We soon found ourselves borrowing to buy carpeting, insulation, storm windows, landscaping, and even a new pick-up truck.*

"Within three years, we were insolvent," Lillian continued.
"Then the worst happened…. My husband lost his job, and our
insolvency was more than inconvenient, it was critical."

People who gave in to the temptation to borrow against their homes in the boom years were far more likely to be underwater when the bubble burst. One study showed that 38 percent of those who had a second mortgage (home equity loan or line of credit) owed more on their homes than they were worth in 2011, compared to just 18 percent of those who had only a single, primary mortgage.

In reality, nobody else—not your lender, your real estate agent, or your relatives—can tell you how much house you can actually handle. That depends on a number of factors that others typically don't know, such as how much you need to save for retirement, how many children you want to have, and how tied down to a house you want to be.

Buying a house today is a lot different than a generation ago, when rampant inflation meant big annual pay raises. Those made a mortgage payment look smaller and smaller as years passed. People back then were also more likely to be covered by a traditional pension, which meant they didn't have to save gobs of money to pay for their retirements. And fewer families had two wage earners, which meant Mom could always go to work if Dad lost his job. Today, many families need both salaries to pay the mortgage, and the loss of one is a disaster.

Those are among the reasons why it's often smart to limit your total housing payments—principle, interest, taxes, and insurance—to 25 percent of your gross monthly income. You might be able to go a bit higher if you have no other debt or a great pension that lessens your need to contribute to your own retirement. You might want to aim a little lower if you plan to have kids and want one spouse to stay home to care for them.

Don't Overdose on Student Loan Debt

Student loans are often referred to as a "good" debt—the kind of borrowing that will increase your earning power and thus more than pay for itself.

Unfortunately, many students are taking a good thing way too far.

Michelle of Indiana emailed to say she owed $120,000 in student loans—and was making just under $50,000 as an assistant professor in her field. She had consolidated all her federal loans and deferred payment when she could, but the cold hard truth was setting in:

"I am staring at a debt that I cannot repay. Our salaries have been
frozen for the next two years due to state budget problems, and I've
calculated that even paying the minimum on all my loans would leave
me with less than 100 dollars to live out the month. Is bankruptcy
my only option? I'm not seeing a way out of this."

I had to give her some news that was even worse than she was expecting. Student loans can almost never be wiped out in bankruptcy court. Federal law requires that student borrowers prove repayment would be an extreme hardship—a tough standard to meet "unless you're totally permanently disabled," in the words of Los Angeles bankruptcy attorney Leon Bayer.

You'll do yourself a huge favor by limiting how much you borrow. Your student loan payments shouldn't total more than 10 percent of your first job's monthly pay. Although how much that lets you borrow depends on the interest rates you'll pay, you can pretty much figure that your total student loan debt shouldn't equal more than that first job's annual pay. It's also smart to limit yourself to federal student loans, which have fixed rates, numerous consumer protections, and the possibility of forgiveness. Private student loans, by contrast, have variable rates, far fewer protections, and no forgiveness options built in. At the very least, exhaust all available federal student loans before considering the private version.

What if you discover that you're already in too deep? If you haven't gotten your degree yet, you can save yourself some pain by transferring to a less-expensive school or taking a year off to work. If you're already out, consider consolidating your federal loans to stretch out the payments. You might even need to work a second job for a while to raise the cash to retire this debt.

Don't Let Your Fixed Expenses Eat Up Your Income

William made a respectable income, yet constantly felt strapped for cash. He wasn't living any higher than his neighbors, he thought, and considerably more frugally than some. So what was wrong?

Like many people, William's fixed expenses had risen along with his pay. He carried a hefty mortgage, along with payments on a nice car, a home equity line of credit, and some student loans. Child care was another big expense, as were groceries, utilities, insurance, and gas. When he actually crunched the numbers, he found more than 70 percent of his take-home pay was going to what he considered his basic, mandatory expenses. When he added in his more-variable expenses—clothing, dinners out, walking-around cash, and so on—he found he was spending more than 90 percent of his take-home pay every month, leaving him precious little breathing room.

That's why Elizabeth Warren, the bankruptcy expert-cum-lawmaker, recommends limiting your fixed, "must-have" expenses to no more than 50 percent of your after-tax income. That way, you can devote 30 percent of your pay to your "wants"—the stuff that's nice if not necessary to have—and 20 percent to savings, which can include the money you use to pay down your debt.

"Must haves," as she details in the book she coauthored, *All Your Worth*, include your housing payments, utilities (including phone and cable or satellite), groceries, insurance, child care, child support, transportation expenses, and minimum payments on your other loans. Trimming those to 50 percent of your after-tax income can be tough, particularly if—like William—you feel you "deserve" to live a certain lifestyle. But doing so, Warren says, can help people finally achieve balance in their lives. They'll have enough money to pay down debt, save for the future, and still have fun once in awhile.

Don't Raid Your Retirement or Your Home Equity to Pay Off Credit Cards

In the boom times, lenders loved to push home equity loans or lines of credit as the "solution" to your debt problems. In fact, these loans often cause more problems than they solve:

- You're draining away the equity that could give you a financial cushion in an emergency. Especially if your savings are meager, you might need to turn to your home equity to help you survive a job loss. How are you going to feel if your equity is already gone?

- More important, you're not dealing with the overspending that got you into credit card debt in the first place. Nearly two-thirds of the people who took out home equity loans between 1996 and 1998 to pay off credit cards had incurred more card debt within two years, according to a study by Atlanta research firm Brittain Associates.

- You're turning unsecured debt, which could be erased in bankruptcy, into debt that's secured by your home. If you can't pay this loan, you could lose your house.

Turning to your retirement funds isn't much better, as I detailed in Chapter 6, "Coping with a Credit Crisis." The taxes and penalties that are due on premature withdrawals will equal up to half of any money you take out. You'll also be missing out on the future tax-deferred returns that money could have made; you should figure that every $10,000 withdrawal costs you at least $100,000 in future retirement income.

Even loans against 401(k)s are risky because you typically have to pay the money back promptly if you lose your job, or the balance will be taxed and penalized as a withdrawal.

A much better course, for most people, is to pay off credit card debt out of current incomes whenever possible. Leave retirement funds for retirement and your home equity, if you have any, for true emergencies.

Credit and Divorce: How Your Ex Can Kill Your Score

Even if you're doing everything right with your own finances, you can still take the fall for someone else's mistakes. Albert, an Army officer, remarried soon after his divorce. However, his ex-wife's sloppy credit habits were still trashing his credit score a decade later:

> *"The problem is that she was not ordered to refinance the house in her name only," Albert wrote. "Since then, she has never made the mortgage payments on time, and it reflects on my credit report. Except for that payment, my present wife and I have perfect credit."*

It's not that his ex can't afford the $263 monthly payment, Albert explained; both she and her second husband have good salaries. She's just habitually late.

Albert contacted the lender and the credit bureaus, all of which gave him the same answer: As long as his name is still on the loan, the payments will continue to show up on his report and affect his credit score.

Many divorced people are shocked to discover that their exes can hurt their credit years after the split is final. Even when a divorce decree clearly spells out that the former spouse is responsible for paying a debt, you can still be on the hook.

That's because creditors don't have to care what a divorce decree says. You made your agreements with lenders well before your divorce, and your lenders didn't have any say in the decree's terms. So if your name is still on the loan, the account was opened jointly, or your spouse was added as an authorized user of a credit card, you can be held responsible.

Some people are in this fix because they didn't use an attorney to help with their divorces, but some did have legal representation—and still weren't alerted to the potential problem.

Many lawyers let couples work out how they're going to handle joint debts on their own, said attorney and financial planner Amy Boohaker of Sarasota, Florida. The attorney might not know, or bother to communicate, the potential ramifications of not shutting down joint credit.

As a result, I regularly get anguished emails from people whose credit report is littered with an ex's delinquencies, charge-offs, collections, and even bankruptcies.

The best time to handle the issue is well before the divorce is final, but you can do some things even afterward. Read on.

Get Your Credit Reports

Identify every credit account that your ex could access. If the account is listed as joint, rather than individual, your spouse can probably use it. If the account is listed as individual and is still open, call the creditor to find out whether your spouse is listed as an authorized user.

Take Action

You might be able to get your spouse removed as an authorized user with a phone call to the card issuer, but follow up in writing.

With joint accounts, your best bet is to close them whenever possible, although you might have to settle for "freezing" the account with the creditor if you owe a balance. (This kind of freeze is supposed to prevent either of you from using the card, which is different from the credit report freezes I detailed in Chapter 5, "Credit-Scoring Myths.")

Unfortunately, though, sometimes a spouse can talk a creditor into lifting a freeze, which is why it's important to put your request in writing, note that you and your spouse are divorcing, and make it clear that you won't be responsible for any charges made after the freeze is in place.

If you do have a balance, it should be transferred as soon as possible to the card of the spouse who will be responsible for paying it off.

What if your spouse can't get credit in his own name? If the divorce isn't final, you might want to take on the debts and get a larger property settlement to offset the extra burden, rather than leave your future credit score in the hands of someone who could so easily trash it.

If the divorce is final, you might need to take over the payments to prevent further damage to your credit rating. Your divorce decree might allow you to take your ex back to court for reimbursement, but either way, you shouldn't leave your credit in his hands for a second longer.

A few months after you make your requests, get another copy of your credit reports to make sure the accounts are listed properly. If an account that was closed is listed as open, or if the balance on a frozen account has grown, follow up immediately with the creditor.

Don't Be Late

Divorce negotiations can drag on almost endlessly, but just one late payment can hurt your credit. You might need to make a few payments on debts that will ultimately be your spouse's, just to make sure they don't go delinquent while you're still responsible for the account.

Dealing with Mortgages, Car Loans, and Other Secured Debt

Ideally, you should either sell the asset and split up the proceeds, or refinance the loan so that you're no longer on the hook. If refinancing is an option, make sure it gets done before the divorce is final.

Sometimes, though, your ex won't want to sell and won't have the income or credit to swing a refinance. If that's the case, set some kind of time limit on how long you're willing to stay on the loan.

If your ex wants to continue living in the family home with your kids, you might agree that the house will be sold when the youngest is 18. Make sure this agreement is part of your divorce decree, and ask the lender to send loan statements and payment coupons to you so that you can make sure the loan is getting paid. At the very least, you should get Internet or phone access to the account so that you can monitor the situation.

If you're already divorced, you might still want to get access to the account and make the payments if your ex is falling behind. Again, your divorce decree might allow you to take him back to court for reimbursement.

If your ex could refinance but won't, you might have to resort to bribes—a cash payment or more time with the kids in exchange for getting a new loan.

Whatever your arrangement, don't sign a quitclaim or let your name be taken off the title as long as your name is still on the loan. You don't want to be responsible for the debt if you no longer own the asset.

Consider a Fraud Alert or Credit Freeze

If you're in a particularly nasty divorce, or if your spouse is unethical, you might wind up a victim of identity theft. After all, your spouse knows your Social Security number, your address, and just about any other detail required to open up a new account in your name, run up a balance, and leave you holding the bag.

Your ex could even file a bankruptcy in your name because many districts don't require identification when a bankruptcy is first filed. By the time the first hearing rolls around, the bankruptcy has already been logged in the huge central database combed by credit bureaus and will show up on your credit report. Such a bogus filing is a crime, but that doesn't prevent some vengeful exes from doing it.

A credit freeze, which prevents anyone from opening an account in your name, is probably the best solution if your state allows it. If not, ask the three credit bureaus to put a fraud alert on your files. You also should get regular copies of your credit reports—at least twice a year—to monitor for anything suspicious.

If a phony bankruptcy has been filed, you'll need to hire a bankruptcy attorney who knows how to get the filing expunged.

In Conclusion: The Three-Year Solution

There's one more issue to address that can have a profound effect on your credit score, your finances, and your life. And that's the issue of how much you can "afford" to borrow on something other than a house or an education.

Many people assume they can afford something if they can make the monthly payments. But that kind of short-term thinking will shackle you to a lifetime of paying interest on stuff that will break, wear out, and become useless long before the last payment is due.

Either that, or you'll trap yourself into an "upside-down" loan.

That's the case for about 80 percent of new car buyers, who drive off the lot owing more on their cars than the vehicles are worth. Many come into dealerships still owing money on their trade-ins, and they compound the problem by taking out five-, six-, or even seven-year loans. Those longer payback periods, combined with the speed in which a new car depreciates, mean they'll stay upside down for years.

The problem? Your car gets totaled, or you lose your job, and you can't get enough for your car to pay off the loan. You'll still owe thousands, and you might be wheel-less besides.

One way to avoid that problem entirely is, of course, to pay cash for everything. This approach has plenty of advocates, and if you understand the power of compound interest, you can see why.

Let's say Ralph decides to buy a car and finance it with a $20,000 loan. At 5 percent interest over five years, Ralph will make 60 payments of $377.42, for a total cost of $22,645.

Jamal, by contrast, decides to save up to buy a car. He invests $294.09 a month for five years at 5 percent interest and ends up with $20,000 cash—but he only contributed $17,645 out of his own pocket. The rest of the money came from interest paid on his savings.

The difference between the two approaches is substantial: Ralph will pay nearly $5,000 more than Jamal.

Many people, though, lack Jamal's discipline. There are so many other demands on their money—and so many tempting things to buy—that the cash never quite gets from their paychecks to the savings accounts.

I hope that as you gain more control over your credit and your finances, you'll become the kind of savvy consumer who can pay cash for a car and other consumer purchases. In the meantime, though, you can save yourself a ton of money and potential hassles with the three-year rule.

By that, I mean not borrowing any amount of money—other than a mortgage or a student loan—that you can't pay back in three years.

A three-year loan means you'll face bigger payments, but you'll pay much less interest now and over your lifetime. You'll also reduce the time you spend "upside down" on your purchase, even if you can't make much of a down payment.

You should consider this approach for many home improvements, as well. Most of the stuff people do to their homes, from remodeling kitchens to adding swimming pools, doesn't add as much value to their houses as the project costs. In other words, the improvements aren't an investment— they're consumption.

Give yourself a three-year payback period, and you'll rein in some of the temptation to overspend. You don't have to go without—you just have to get realistic about costs.

What's the reward for all this hard work, discipline, and restraint? Greater wealth, greater freedom, and a greater ability to get the loans you need, when you need them, at the best possible rates.

Instead of being at lenders' mercy, you'll be the one in charge.

And wasn't that the whole reason for reading this book in the first place? Instead of being turned down for credit or paying too much for it, you've learned the best ways to fix, improve, and protect your score so that you can qualify for the best rates and terms. You've learned to separate fact from fiction when it comes to credit scoring and discovered the fastest ways to rebuild after a financial disaster.

You've realized that you don't have to feel helpless or outgunned by creditors. By learning how credit and credit scoring work, you've taken back the power to manage your finances. May that knowledge help you build the life you want.

Index

DISCARD